AF767019

SWINDON TOWN'S

JOURNEY TO THE PREMIER LEAGUE

The PITCH Report

Love great sportswriting? So do we.

Every month, Pitch Publishing brings together the best of our world through our monthly newsletter – a space for readers, writers and fans to connect over the books, people and moments that make sport so captivating.

You'll find previews of new releases, extracts from our latest titles, behind-the-scenes interviews with authors and the occasional giveaway or competition thrown in for good measure.

We also dip into our back catalogue to unearth forgotten gems and celebrate timeless tales that shaped sporting culture.

Scan the **QR code** and join the growing Pitch Publishing reader community today.

David Wallis

SWINDON TOWN'S JOURNEY TO THE PREMIER LEAGUE

The Robins' Incredible Rise to the Top

pitch

First published by Pitch Publishing, 2026
1

Pitch Publishing
9 Donnington Park, 85 Birdham Road
Chichester, West Sussex, PO20 7AJ
www.pitchpublishing.co.uk
info@pitchpublishing.co.uk

© 2026, David Wallis

The moral right of the author and illustrator has been asserted in accordance with the Copyright, Designs and Patents Act 1988

Every effort has been made to trace the copyright. Any oversight will be rectified in future editions at the earliest opportunity by the publisher.

No part of this book may be used or reproduced in any manner for the purpose of training artificial intelligence technologies or systems. In accordance with Article 4(3) of the DSM Directive 2019/790, Pitch Publishing expressly reserves this work from the text and data mining exception.

Set in Adobe Caslon 11.3/16pt

Typeset by Pitch Publishing

Cover design by Olner Design

Printed and bound in India by Thomson Press India Private Limited

The authorised representative in the EEA is
Easy Access System Europe OÜ, Mustamäe tee 50, 10621 Tallinn, Estonia gpsr.requests@easproject.com

A CIP catalogue record for this book is available from the British Library

ISBN 978-1-83680-443-7

Papers used by Pitch Publishing are from well-managed forests and other responsible sources

MIX
Paper | Supporting responsible forestry
FSC® C010615

Contents

Foreword by Paul Bodin

I AM hugely indebted to Lou Macari for bringing me to Swindon Town in 1988 and I'd really like to thank him for doing so. He recruited some fantastic players over his time. I probably didn't play too much under Lou, but it was Ossie Ardiles who really gave me a platform to perform and who showed huge confidence in me. His style of play really suited me.

It was like total football, ahead of its time and using the diamond formation which I'd never seen before. He identified the players, and he knew how to get the best out of them.

Colin Calderwood excelled under Ossie and went on to play for Scotland. Alan McLoughlin behind the front two was given the responsibility to use his intelligence and receiving abilities, and his wonderful two-footed skills led to his own international honours. Ossie allowed us all to express ourselves and got the best out of us.

After Lou left, everyone had to change, including the supporters' mindsets. Ossie certainly brought the best out of me and everyone. We were all comfortable in possession and enjoyed the transformation.

It was a great team, and we all complemented each other. The squads were much smaller then, which allowed the young players coming through to shine. Ossie's man-management was terrific. He was such a humble man to lead Swindon Town.

When Glenn Hoddle arrived, he wanted to continue his playing career, and the role of sweeper was perfect for him. That allowed him to play behind a back three with Ross MacLaren offering the insurance of a holding role in front, like a back four diamond.

Big Shaun Taylor arrived; he could play some wonderful balls with his left foot, and partnered Colin, who had improved so much under Ossie as a ball-playing centre-half. And then Glenn had such incredible ability that it all helped the unity of the team to become even better, and the slightly different formation allowed us to be more flexible.

The different setup of a 3-5-2 allowed the full-backs to express ourselves. It was a really strong, attacking threat down the wings, which also freed up space in the middle for Martin Ling and John Moncur, and with Glenn's passing range we could switch play in an instant.

All the players and our families socialised in Swindon and there was a great camaraderie and affinity with the supporters.

Ossie's side that was demoted in 1990 would have been well equipped to retain their top-flight place, because the players remained. The biggest problem we had in 1993 was losing such key players as Dave Mitchell and Colin, and of course Glenn, who was our leader both on and off the pitch. If we had kept those three, I believe we would have retained our Premier League place. Those key players were sorely missed.

John Gorman was a wonderful manager and an unflappable man who wore his heart on his sleeve and was very thorough. He had the difficult task of guiding us through a tough and enjoyable season in the Premier League.

International striker Jan-Åge Fjørtoft from Norway came in and found it tough to score for the first six months, but once he got going he was an incredible goal machine. To reach the Premier League was an incredible achievement. We couldn't stay there, but all the players and supporters have wonderful memories.

Paul Bodin
Swindon Town 1988–1991; 1992–1996

Introduction

The Way We Were

AS THE 20th century passed into the final decade of the millennium, global change was gathering pace.

Tim Berners-Lee's vision of the world wide web saw the light of day. Acid rain and ozone layer depletion had the world fretting. Global warming initially appeared to herald more picnics in the park, before becoming a portent of environmental disaster. We learned that the Amazon was the lungs of the planet, and later it was a global distributor of the written word.

The new development of the unfettered phone, initially in the guise of the 'car phone' and often subsequently described as a 'brick' as it attempted improved portability, was transformed from an image of envy to one of scorn, as the media parodied the Yuppie into ridicule. The mobile reduced in dimensions, as it grew to become indispensable by all.

Nelson Mandela, the future president of South Africa, walked free from jail after 27 years of incarceration. The poll tax riots had taken place in the UK, Margaret Thatcher resigned as prime minister and recession took hold.

Globally, the fall of the Berlin Wall redefined the map of Europe. We discovered that *Glasnost* was not a Moscow

Dynamo central defender, and we learned that *Perestroika* was not Russian for 'a pair of strikers'.

Meanwhile on the eastern fringe of the West Country, the town of Swindon, founded on the heavy industry of the development of railway, was being forced to adapt and adopt.

Adapt, as the vast steam engine manufacturing works which had been dominant for 150 years were forced into closure. Adopt, as the influx of high-tech and financial businesses to the borough brought about the oft-used description of 'the fastest growing town in Europe'.

If there was to be a major split throughout society and industry, Swindon looked like being on the prosperous side of the great divide.

In football too, huge change was about to be unveiled. The Premier League had been mooted for years, and finally an inauguration date of 1992 was announced.

Also, as the dawn of the 1990s crept toward the horizon, Swindon Town Football Club had been undergoing its own seismic change.

The appointment of Manchester United legend Lou Macari as player-manager in 1984 had seen great strides as the Scot dragged the club from the lower reaches of the Fourth Division to the brink of the promised land of the First Division, before departing for West Ham United in the summer of 1989 and leaving Swindon tantalisingly close to the top flight.

Macari had been hailed as a messiah as he did so much to redefine Swindon's place in football's pecking order. Lifting the club up through three divisions had culminated in falling just short of completing the task of leading the Wiltshire club to the promised land of the pre-Premier League First Division.

On 19 July 1989, Tottenham Hotspur and Argentina's World Cup-winning midfield maestro Ossie Ardiles was appointed as Town's new player-manager, and a new era beckoned. In the popular vernacular, 'The King was dead. Long live the King.'

A new adventure was about to begin, one which would bring success and heartbreak in similar measure.

1

1989/90

THE APPOINTMENT of Osvaldo Ardiles as player-manager of Swindon Town immediately appeared an inspired move by the board of directors.

Bristol Rovers boss Gerry Francis, the former England international midfielder, was among those who had reportedly interested the board, while Cardiff City manager Frank Burrows – a former Swindon centre-back – had also been rumoured to be in the frame. But both had been overlooked in favour of Ardiles.

Having made such an excellent decision by recruiting Lou Macari in the summer of 1984, the directors and everyone associated with the club had been rewarded with an unprecedented five-season run which had lifted Swindon from the lower reaches of the Fourth Division to the very threshold of the First Division.

Falling just short of promotion through a defeat inflicted by Crystal Palace in the 1988/89 play-off semi-finals, Macari had felt he had lifted the club as high as he could and he moved on to West Ham United. By appointing another midfielder of the highest pedigree as his replacement, it was hoped that Ossie Ardiles could complete the job.

The 36-year-old took the reins for his first managerial position, so there was an inevitable element of risk that the

Argentinian might not be able to transfer his footballing philosophies to his new charges. But the same chance had been taken with Macari five years earlier with spectacular success.

On the announcement of Ardiles's appointment, chairman Brian Hillier said in the *Swindon Evening Advertiser*, 'With any appointment nobody can guarantee it will be a success, but you make the decision and try to make it work. He's got an exceptional footballing background, he's ambitious and hard-working enough to be successful as a football manager.'

Hillier later advised that it had been Ardiles who had made the first approach regarding the vacancy.

Meanwhile, ex-Tottenham Hotspur man Ardiles commented, 'I am delighted that Swindon have asked me to be their manager and I am very excited about the prospect. Swindon are an ambitious club and I hope to take them into the First Division.'

Holder of a World Cup winners' medal for Argentina after his performance in the 1978 final, the Córdoba-born star came from a family of lawyers, and it was initially assumed Ardiles would follow his father and sibling into the legal business. Studying law at university, a move to Buenos Aires put his studies on hold more than four years into a six-year course as his football aspirations took over.

Ardiles's playing contract had also been secured for Town. A broken leg sustained in his last match for Queens Park Rangers the previous January had led him to join Fort Lauderdale Strikers in the US as he recovered from injury, and the Florida-based club had released him so that he could take up his new appointment.

With Town in the Second Division and benefiting from the shrewd recruitment of Macari's tenure, the playing staff was a very different kettle of fish than that inherited by the Scot five seasons previously. Ardiles did not really need the wholesale player cull and replacement that his predecessor had felt necessary in 1984.

Even so, there was more than the odd raised eyebrow when Ardiles announced that he intended to change Swindon's playing style to one which the purists may have considered easier on the eye.

Macari had achieved success through hard work, fitness and camaraderie, and there had been criticism that his team's style was a little too functional. As much as it could be expected that Ardiles would prefer his side to play with the panache so long demonstrated by the man himself, was the playing staff of sufficient quality for him to instil his demands on the training field? And could the club fund the recruitment that Ardiles might reasonably demand if it was found wanting?

If the answer to both these questions was 'no', would the task of leading Town to greater things be beyond the new man?

Pre-season in Wiltshire started in traditional manner as Swindon toured local non-league clubs in search of a workout and a chance to put new training ground procedures into practice. Triallists and youngsters were offered the chance to earn contracts, established squad members were tried in unfamiliar positions and new haircuts confused the watching fans.

A first outing at nearby Calne resulted in a perfunctory 7-1 win for the visiting professionals. Similar fixtures around the locality produced similar outcomes and allowed new free-kick routines to see the light of day. Goodwill was generated around the county as welcome cash flowed into the smaller clubs' coffers, and big names took to the newly manicured pitches of clubs further down the pyramid.

While the standard of opposition ramped up as the big kick-off approached, to include teams supplied by Tottenham Hotspur and West Ham, Swindon went through their campaign undefeated.

Results of such encounters are usually considered inconsequential, but 32 goals scored against nine conceded is the sort of return that would encourage some feelgood factor anyway. Town's goalscorers were finding the net, defenders were honing their partnerships and things looked rosy as the season loomed.

Ardiles appeared encouraged as he introduced himself through the pages of the *Evening Advertiser.* 'I want my players to play, play, play,' he said in reply to questions regarding the style he would demand of his team. 'Obviously I do not expect to change Swindon's style overnight. After all, it has brought great success.'

Elsewhere, Ossie said, 'Swindon got very close to the First Division last season, and I will not want to change that successful side yet. I would like to encourage the players to develop their skills.'

In other comments, he added, 'Football is not black and white. The style you play depends on the players at your disposal, but I will try to bring in as much football as I can. The best football is a mixture of long and short ball.'

After the behind-closed-doors friendly with Spurs, left-back Phil King ruefully offered, 'We did more passing today than we've done in the past few years.'

As the opening game of the season approached, Ardiles's first piece of transfer business took place. Conjuring up thoughts of old partnerships, the boss persuaded Sheffield Wednesday to part with his former Tottenham Hotspur team-mate Tony Galvin on a free transfer.

The midfielder had obtained a BA in Russian from Hull University, and fittingly he was to take up a position on the left.

Until then, all significant transfer dealings had been outgoings. Ardiles had previously commented, 'I want to study the players we have here, so we will start the season with roughly the same squad and see how it goes. I'm pleased with the condition of the players. Most of them look quite fit.'

But as if to emphasise the coming of a new era, two former stars of the Macari-led surge through the divisions, Charlie Henry and Peter Coyne, took their goalscoring contributions elsewhere.

Henry made a short move to Aldershot, and while Coyne initially took the same trip on loan, the striker eventually joined Colne Dynamos instead. Between them the pair had contributed 16 seasons of service to Swindon's progression through the Football League, claiming more than 70 goals.

On 19 August 1989 Swindon took to the County Ground pitch for the first competitive fixture under the leadership of Ardiles. Sunderland were the visitors for the Second Division match that day and the team line-up featured new signing Galvin. The boss named himself as a substitute.

In his programme notes, Ossie said, 'There will be few prouder managers in the Football League than myself when 3pm arrives today. It is an honour to be manager of an English club and I will always be grateful to Swindon Town for the opportunity. After a few weeks I can say I am very pleased with the squad of players I have found here at Swindon Town. Their attitude is excellent. They will find me a man who expects dedication and full effort. There is a lot of skill amongst the players and that is very pleasing. I will change the style slightly. Players must be encouraged to feel comfortable with the ball and to use their skills.'

The occasion, however, did not bring about the start that everyone connected with the home side would have hoped for. After two goals conceded and none scored, it was the Wearsiders who returned north with the three points.

Midfielder Fitzroy Simpson was sent off two minutes into the second half for back-chatting at referee Tony Ward. Ardiles came off the bench to replace Galvin on the hour, and the boss also entered Ward's book in added time for not retreating at a free kick. It was not the greatest of introductions.

In his following programme notes, Ossie described the outcome as 'a minor setback, but one we can learn a lesson from. You can always learn more in defeat than in victory.'

Better was to come, but it was not to be immediate. And the name Sunderland would be writ large in the club's history before the end of the season.

Seven games in came the biggest reverse so far, and it would be the largest margin of defeat that Town suffered in the entire campaign. A trip to Elland Road on 23 September to face Leeds United resulted in a 4-0 defeat.

Swindon went down to ten men just after the hour when Jon Gittens left United's John Hendrie needing five stitches to a shin injury, but by the time the defender departed the field his team were already two goals behind.

It was Hendrie who referee George Courtney decided was unfairly upended by Simpson, and the resultant penalty was successfully tucked past goalkeeper Fraser Digby's left hand by Gordon Strachan to give the home side a 15th-minute lead.

By half-time Strachan had already added a second, and after Gittens' red card, Bobby Davison scored the Whites' third. The mercurial Strachan then completed his hat-trick with a fourth in injury time.

The match had been an eye-opening demonstration of the quality of opposition Ardiles's side would face. Town had finished four places above Leeds the previous season, but on the day the home side were vastly superior and by the end of the afternoon were fourth in the table, while Swindon were 21st.

The eventual champions would only once occupy a place lower in the table before the season's end as they went on to claim the trophy. Thankfully Swindon's momentum was only upward from that day too with Ardiles getting the full idea of what his side were to face.

Between the opening-day defeat to Sunderland and the mauling at Elland Road, Swindon had not been setting the table alight. A 2-2 draw at Oldham Athletic was followed by the first win, a convincing 3-1 at home to Wolverhampton Wanderers.

By then, supporters had already seen the last of Ardiles the player. By the end of August, and with Ardiles restricting himself to just a substitute appearance in each of the first two games of the season, the South American legend called time on his pitch-based activities.

When a trip to Upton Park pitched Ossie's side against departed Lou Macari's West Ham, there was pride at stake as well as three points. Could Swindon outdo their old boss and demonstrate a successful changing of the guard?

In the event, honours were shared. Gittens netted a 53rd-minute equaliser to cancel out Martin Allen's opener and while the draw knocked West Ham off the top of the early Second Division table, two evenly matched sides produced a competitive encounter in which Town arguably finished the stronger.

Fraser Digby was adjudged to have been the star of the show, sustaining a cut to his face when making a brave early stop and following that up with several more crucial saves before crowning his display in the final minute with a vital, point-retaining, two-handed block from Mark Ward. Lou Macari told the *Evening Advertiser*, 'That save must have made Fraser's day. He had a tremendous game.'

Just days later, it was revealed that Macari had enquired about Digby's availability, and with the goalkeeper already considering a new contract offer he had plainly timed his approach well. It was Macari himself, while in charge at the County Ground, who had placed a price of £800,000 on Digby's head only the previous season.

But by the end of the week the Scot had been told that Digby was not for sale, even at the price he himself had put in place.

The return match was scheduled to pit Ardiles and Macari against each other at the County Ground the following February. The game would take place; the contest between the two bosses wouldn't.

Defeat at Sheffield United and a goalless draw at home to the Blades' fellow Yorkshire side Barnsley rounded off the first month of the season with no extra goals scored, and only one point gained.

After five seasons of unbridled success under Macari, this was not what Town supporters had been hoping for when his successor had been appointed in the summer, and the convincing defeat at Leeds a week later compounded their disappointment.

Striker Shaun Close had been added to the playing ranks when Ardiles spent £70,000 on the Bournemouth man. Ardiles had said in the programme, 'I have known Shaun from our days at Tottenham Hotspur and he proved to be a natural goalscorer. Shaun will be a valuable asset to Swindon Town when he has settled in.'

But things were about to turn for the better, and the turnaround burst into life with a tempestuous 3-0 midweek home win over Plymouth Argyle.

Tom Jones grabbed the first, eight minutes before half-time. His quick header caught the visiting goalkeeper Rhys Wilmot out, as his previous ball aimed at Duncan Shearer was cleared. Then when Shearer was replaced by substitute Tony Galvin the momentum swung towards the home side.

Phil King added a second goal with an exquisite 77th-minute 25-yard chip over Wilmot's head after a superb ball from Galvin, and the scoring was completed by Paul Bodin, who had replaced Jones and cracked in an 87th-minute drive.

But there was far more incident than suggested by the scoresheet.

The game also contained a double sending-off six minutes into the second half, when Close walked along with Argyle's David Byrne after an off-the-ball incident involving both men.

Then 18-year-old Fitzroy Simpson tangled with the away side's right-back Kenny Brown. Again, two cards were shown, but the Town youngster saw red while Brown's was yellow.

One goal apiece and nine men versus ten. Then came the introduction of Bodin and Galvin and the outcome was ripe for a breathless conclusion. An incredible point-blank save from Digby with the score at 2-0 had kept the defence unbroken to complete a good evening's work.

Perhaps the rest of the season had begun to be redefined. Swindon had overcome adversity, proved the depth of the squad, claimed only their second clean sheet of the season and shown that there were goals throughout the team.

Ardiles seemed appreciative of the performances of those of the diminished numbers on the field. 'I would like to pay tribute to the nine players who were left to ensure our win. Paul Bodin and Tony Galvin were magnificent,' he said, although he did add, 'I was tremendously disappointed that Shaun Close was elbowed and retaliated.'

It might be a little over-analytical to wonder whether there had been a eureka moment, but had the players realised that individually they were capable of more than the hard-working game that had been so successful under Lou Macari? That maybe, collectively, they could build on their previous strengths and add an extra, Ardiles-inspired ingredient that could build on the achievements of the past?

Whatever the reasoning behind it, the result against Argyle and the nature of the performance which brought it about appeared to herald a significant change in fortune, because six of the next eight Second Division matches would bring three-point hauls. Over those seven weeks, Swindon rose from a relegation-threatening 21st in the table to a play-off position of fifth.

The turnaround continued with an away trip to Bradford City. A goal by Steve White five minutes from time equalised

City man Mark Aizlewood's finish just six minutes earlier, which had come from a self-inflicted mistake.

Fraser Digby had raced out of goal to intercept a long ball aimed towards ex-Town striker Jim Quinn. But the Northern Ireland international won the race and his cross to the vacant goal was met by the brother of former Swindon man Steve Aizlewood, who headed home and appeared to have clinched the game for the home team.

Then in the 85th minute White pounced on a loose ball to drive past Paul Tomlinson in the City goal to share the points. White had been a half-time substitute for Alan McLoughlin, who was struggling with a flu virus, while summer signing Tony Galvin had made his last start for the Robins.

Mistakes notwithstanding, the draw was the least that Town deserved on the day. Stalwart *Evening Advertiser* reporter Clive King noticed the attention of a Manchester United scout, who was said to have been checking on the form of Town left-back Phil King.

But wordsmith King suggested that United's attention may have been more drawn to the performance of young midfielder Fitzroy Simpson.

As for Town's scorer that day, Steve White's goal was his 50th since joining on a free transfer from Bristol Rovers three years previously.

Chipping Sodbury-born 'Chalkie' had started his career at Mangotsfield United and joined Second Division Bristol Rovers in 1977. After a season when the striker recorded almost a goal every other match, successive and successful moves to Luton Town and Charlton Athletic allowed the former England schoolboy international to retain his divisional status as Rovers dropped into the Third Division.

Over more than 90 appearances at Kenilworth Road and then The Valley, White claimed close to another 40 strikes, so it comes as somewhat of a surprise that in August 1983 he was allowed to return to the West Country and Eastville, despite scoring 12 times in 29 outings for Athletic the previous season.

And if that seems as though Steve wasn't being full appreciated, it's even more mystifying that he was snapped up on a free transfer in July 1986 for Swindon by Lou Macari, despite scoring a further 24 times over 89 appearances in his second spell at Bristol Rovers.

Steve's own recollections cast an interesting perspective later in the book.

Whatever it was that made White undervalued at all his three previous clubs, there was no disguising the fact that he turned out to be the subject of one of the most astute pieces of transfer business ever carried out by Swindon.

On 3 October, a meeting of the two STFCs saw the Wiltshire version paired against that of Shropshire as Swindon faced Shrewsbury Town at the County Ground in the second leg of the League Cup second round. A comfortable 3-0 away victory in September was compounded by a 3-1 success a fortnight later to see Swindon through to round three, which would produce a tie which was far more convoluted.

Back in the Second Division, a trip to Hull brought a meeting against a City side struggling at the wrong end of the table. Nine games in, the Tigers had yet to record a win. Meanwhile, Swindon had begun a tentative sally up the table, but were still looking for their first away victory.

Jon Gittens was serving a suspension following his dismissal against Leeds two weeks earlier. That opened up an opportunity for Tim Parkin to make a return to the starting line-up and he marked the occasion with the 75th-minute goal which earned Swindon maximum points.

There were suggestions that Parkin's goal might have been somewhat fortunate. A Jones cross was fumbled by the City goalkeeper Gavin Kelly, and the centre-back was on hand to redirect the ball with his knee. Right-back Neil Buckley hooked it away but referee Stephen Lodge ruled that it had crossed the line.

Parkin, though, had no doubts, 'I saw the keeper was struggling and knew he was about to drop the ball. I couldn't get my foot up to it, and I couldn't get my head down to it, so I just put my knee into it.'

Hull had spent a wretched 21 games searching for a win, going back to the previous season, but with a Town resurgence still in its fragile infancy, an away victory, while by no means assured, was hugely welcome.

Twice forced to come from behind, the Robins had benefitted from equalisers from Simpson and McLoughlin before Parkin's knee claimed all three points, but the credit for the win was claimed to lay with Ardiles's tactical substitutions.

At half-time with Swindon 2-1 behind, Ardiles brought on Jones for King and pushed Paul Bodin back from midfield to the left side of defence.

Bodin was still trying to establish a permanent role within the side having spent time in a variety of midfield positions since joining in March 1988, but the Welshman's move to left-back that day would prove to be a pivotal moment in his career.

Within a month the sought-after King had clinched a £400,000 move to Sheffield Wednesday, Bodin was installed as his permanent replacement at left-back and the man known as 'Zippy' was on his way to full international honours.

A more immediate international call-up came for Fraser Digby, who travelled to Poland to join the England under-21 squad. Nigel Martyn of Bristol Rovers had pulled out as a previous knee ligament injury resurfaced, and 21-year-old Digby, who had already made four under-21 appearances, stepped in as an over-aged player. He helped his country to a 3-1 victory in Jastrzębie.

Back home, the win at Hull had started October in celebratory mood, and over the next ten days the good vibes would continue. The following week saw a convincing 3-0 home victory over Ipswich Town and one man was particularly pleased to make the scoresheet.

Duncan Shearer, the previous season's top scorer, had not found the net in the league for seven games. His 33rd-minute strike opened the scoring and set Swindon on their way to their third win in four matches.

But it was Digby who again stole the show and prevented the scoreline from indicating a far more even encounter. Multiple outstanding saves kept Town's clean sheet unsullied, and his performance was crowned by a 55th-minute penalty stop from Romeo Zondervan after referee Martin Bodenham reckoned Colin Calderwood had fouled Louie Donowa.

The result lifted Swindon to 12th in a tight Second Division table, two points behind Blackburn Rovers who occupied the last play-off place.

Then when Shearer's strike partner Steve White grabbed a brace in another 3-0 win, this time at home to old rivals Oxford United, Town had won three on the trot and taken 13 points of the most recent 15 on offer.

The front two, so prolific in previous years under Lou Macari, had overcome a strangely barren start to the season and got back to their old goalscoring ways.

There was a setback on 21 October when a 2-1 defeat at the home of Leicester City brought the five-match unbeaten run to an end. The Filberts, who were in transition to the Foxes at the time, had made a dismal start to the campaign, hitting the bottom of the table in September and staying there for a month. The win lifted them up a place.

Then it was business as usual when Town travelled to the south coast to face Brighton & Hove Albion at the Goldstone Ground on the first day of November.

An 85th-minute goal from the restored Jon Gittens confirmed that all three points would be on their way back to Wiltshire. Ross MacLaren had opened the scoring with his first goal of the season on 32 minutes, before the Seagulls equalised five minutes into the second half. The win lifted Town up to eighth and there was still more good news to come.

Stoke City's visit to the County Ground a day before Guy Fawkes night saw the arrival of a Potteries side who were not having a happy time of it, with only goal difference keeping them outside the relegation places. Managed by Mick Mills, the ex-England defender had recently appointed World Cup winner Alan Ball to assist him, and on the day there would be pyrotechnics that the treacherous traitor would have been proud of.

Braces for Shearer and White, coupled with an opener from McLoughlin, made sure of consecutive victories, and the own goal scored by ex-Swindon man Dave Bamber two minutes into the second half ensured a 6-0 win for the home side. It was the biggest league win for Town since December 1979 and lifted the Robins to seventh in the table.

With a healthy dose of irony, the visiting supporters started cheering each goal as they realised that the greater the margin of defeat the greater the likelihood that the unpopular Mills would be 'sacked in the morning'. Three days later they got their way.

A week later Swindon were on the road again, this time with the long haul up to Middlesbrough. Boro, still at Ayresome Park, were another team struggling for points and Town took advantage of their bad form with a 2-0 win. Clive King of the *Evening Advertiser* described the performance as 'without doubt Town's best result so far this season'. It lifted Swindon up one more position and into the play-off places.

Over the nine league matches since the drubbing by Leeds back on 23 September, Swindon had won seven, accumulating 22 points, while scoring 24 goals and conceding six. The run had lifted them from 21st to sixth.

In his programme notes, Ossie Ardiles conveyed his satisfaction, 'Tremendous. I am sure that is the correct word to describe our performances in recent weeks. We have shown all the required habits of the British professional player. To say recent results have made me a very happy man is an understatement.'

And talking specifically about the recent demolition of Stoke, he said, 'Some of the moves we produced were breathtaking, and the final score and performance left me feeling a very proud man.'

The boss was pleased, and so were the watching supporters. Meanwhile, a saga had taken place in the third round of the League Cup. The tie had commenced in the fourth week of October and would run for a month.

Drawn at home to Third Division Bolton Wanderers on 24 October, Swindon were denied a passage to the fourth round by a last-minute goal from future County Ground manager Phil Brown. The late drama was the climax to a frenetic match which saw Town twice fight back from behind and still lead 3-2 with seconds to go.

In the days when cup replays weren't considered the undesirable commodity that they would become, a rematch at Burnden Park was set for 7 November, and with the prize for victory known to be a home tie against First Division Southampton, even extra time couldn't separate the two sides, who played out a 1-1 draw.

A toss of the coin decided the venue for a second replay, and it was back to Bolton a week later. Burnden was becoming a burden.

Steve White scored the 150th goal of his career and if that seems decisive, the score after another 120 minutes was another 1-1 stalemate, with the striker ending up in hospital to have eight stitches in a nasty head wound.

So, on to the fourth match, this time back at the County Ground as Southampton kicked their heels in anticipation.

At 90 minutes, incredibly the score stood at 1-1 once more. White, battling through the pain barrier, had given Town the lead just before the hour only for the visitors to hit back once more ten minutes later. Extra time was necessary for the third time.

Finally, with just three minutes of the extra 30 remaining, Ross MacLaren concluded the epic tie with a 22-yard drive which found its way through a crowd of players to give Swindon a 2-1 victory.

The marathon encounter had taken over seven hours to complete and had seen a total attendance of more than

45,000 supporters over the four games. One day football's authorities would decide that even one replay in cup competition was too many, and that the gate-induced extra income was unnecessary.

Just one week later Swindon and Southampton played out a goalless draw at the County Ground, and despite goals from McLoughlin and White at The Dell, after the passage of a further 47 days and yet another 30 minutes of extra time the Saints emerged 4-2 victors.

But trouble was on the horizon, and in the middle of November a story broke that would start a chain of events that would have the most serious repercussions imaginable. Sunday newspaper *The People* ran a story alleging that Town chairman Brian Hillier had placed a bet on his side to lose an FA Cup tie at Newcastle United back in 1988.

That Second Division Town had capitulated 5-0 to the First Division giants was the sort of margin that might have attracted attention, but rather than any suggestion that the outcome had been influenced by the potential financial windfall, the biggest issue was deemed to be that, in placing the wager, the club had breached FA rules designed to prohibit such actions.

Announcing the intention to launch a full inquiry, the FA's investigation would run for months and ultimately wreck the outcome of this season and beyond.

Back in Second Division action, a hugely successful seven weeks had done wonders for Town's position, but such a run was always destined to end and the downturn started at Port Vale on 18 November. It would be a full calendar month before they would taste victory again and it is impossible to determine just how much the FA's announcement influenced performances.

A 2-0 defeat at Vale Park was followed a week later with a Shearer double, but that only produced a point at home against Portsmouth. As December began, goals from McLoughlin and Shearer at Roker Park helped to partially atone for Sunderland's opening-day win at the County Ground with another 2-2 draw.

Town's excellent overall performance on Wearside more than deserved a three-point return, but with the game in injury time, home substitute Thomas Hauser's mishit shot found its way through Digby's legs and two points were lost.

After such a point-strewn haul throughout autumn, two from nine could only be considered a disappointment, and a 3-2 defeat at home to lowly Bournemouth in an error-riddled showing did nothing to lift morale.

'We made far too many mistakes all over the field. Bournemouth exploited them as we gave away three bad goals,' said Ossie Ardiles, continuing, 'Our midfield was non-existent and the only pleasing thing was that we fought until the end.'

A 2-0 loss at home to top-of-the-table Sheffield United five days later continued the downward direction, as Town failed to demonstrate their credentials against the form team of the Second Division. The loss dropped them down to ninth in the table and the season appeared to be slipping away.

So, when a trip to The Hawthorns produced a 2-1 win against West Bromwich Albion courtesy of goals from Shearer and White, Ardiles surely had reason to be more upbeat.

But, incredibly, Town were two goals to the good with an hour gone when referee Ffrangcon Roberts from Prestatyn decided he needed to become the star of the show. Colin

Calderwood and Baggies defender Chris Whyte met for a ball in the Town penalty box on 70 minutes, both ended up on the floor and Roberts pointed to the penalty spot. But Digby dived excellently to his left to push Bernard McNally's spot kick around the post.

From the resultant corner, the cleared ball fell back to McNally who shot at goal, only for it to strike Shearer's hand. Penalty again, said Roberts. And this time Graham Harbey stepped up to blast his shot high over the bar.

Then, only six minutes after the first penalty had been awarded, a linesman indicated to the man in the middle that Jon Gittens had fouled Don Goodman and the busy Roberts needed no persuasion to point to the spot for the third time. This time Goodman tried his luck, and finally Digby was a beaten man.

Ossie was circumspect, 'I do not wish to comment on the penalties, but I will say that I was proud that my players did not react or lose concentration.'

The win heralded the start of the second turnaround of the season for Swindon. Having started the campaign in unconvincing style, it took until the end of September before a rich seam of form had carried them towards the play-off places. Then a run of five games which brought just two points threatened to undo all the hard work.

Blackburn Rovers came to Wiltshire on Boxing Day. They and the Robins had spent much of the previous couple of months challenging each other for a play-off spot, something that would continue to the end of the season.

The game was a festive goal-fest with the two teams sharing seven between them, and Town emerged as the beneficiaries.

Digby was responsible for the 4-3 scoreline not being even higher, even though Town's keeper was beaten twice in the first 20 minutes, the second being an Andy Kennedy penalty which he just failed to keep out.

Shearer reduced the arrears when he successfully blocked an attempted clearance with a little over half an hour gone and saw the ball sail over Rovers keeper Darren Collier into the net. If that was a lucky break, there was no fortune in Shearer's second, when he looped home a header three minutes before the interval for his 16th goal of the season.

By then Digby had been performing heroics in the face of a plethora of Blackburn goalscoring opportunities, but Town still had time to enter the half-time dressing room with the upper hand when Paul Bodin hit an unstoppable shot to give them the lead.

With fog descending on the County Ground, Digby continued in inspired form, making three brilliant stops to prevent Rovers reclaiming parity, but he couldn't prevent a 73rd-minute equaliser from substitute Howard Gayle. But with visibility continuing to deteriorate, Steve Foley forced the ball through a forest of legs to bring the Christmas cracker to a breathless conclusion.

The recovery was under way.

Consecutive victories were followed by a 1-1 draw at Newcastle as Shearer again made the scoresheet. The top-scoring striker had just added an extra two years to his contract. 'I thought about it a bit, but there was never any real doubt in my mind. I've never been happier at the club and my family are very settled here,' he said.

On New Year's Day 1990, Alan McLoughlin grabbed two goals at Watford as Swindon returned home with three points and moved up to fifth. Even an exit from the FA

Cup at Third Division near neighbours Bristol City failed to dampen spirits overly. Ardiles said afterwards, 'We were dismissed from the FA Cup last week because we started to compete and play at too late a stage of the game. We were second best in the first half. We have played well this season, and this particular match will serve as a useful reminder that a match is of 90 minutes' duration.'

Another goal from McLoughlin, added to a pair from White, brought a home win over Oldham, then a narrow defeat at Wolves, despite another White goal, brought the first league defeat in almost six weeks.

It would be almost another two months before Town left the field pointless again, but it would take all of Ardiles's managerial nous to keep his players concentrating on pitch matters.

Because in mid-January the Football League announced that it too would be making investigations into the dealings of the club, after another newspaper story alleged that 'under the counter' payments had been made to players.

Swindon's secretary was sacked as board members searched for the 'mole' within the club, as was reported in the *Evening Advertiser*, and acrimonious allegations were aired. All these developments happened after the FA announced that it was charging Brian Hillier and Lou Macari with misconduct as a result of its own investigations into the alleged bet placed before the 1988 match at Newcastle.

As the story continued to develop, Hillier explained that the bet had been placed as a form of insurance to mitigate against the cost of hotel expenses for the trip to the north-east.

Amidst all this turmoil, Ardiles managed to keep his players focused sufficiently to avenge the huge September defeat by Leeds when the Whites were beaten 3-2 at the County Ground as February commenced.

Howard Wilkinson's side arrived as the Second Division leaders, but left without any points when McLoughlin, man of the match Steve Foley and Ross MacLaren scored the goals that claimed victory. The treble meant that Town had scored 52 league goals already, more than any other club in the Second Division, and lifted them up to third in the table.

And still the points kept coming; skipper Colin Calderwood headed the only goal of the match at Barnsley on 10 February, then followed the long-awaited return of Lou Macari when West Ham arrived at the County Ground.

But Macari was nowhere to be seen.

On 12 February the FA announced that it had found him and Hillier guilty of breaking gambling rules. Hillier was suspended from football involvement for six months and Macari was fined. Under the circumstances, Macari offered his resignation to West Ham and it was announced that he had walked away from the east London club. Both men declared their intentions to appeal the decisions as Swindon considered their options regarding a replacement chairman.

Back on the pitch, a 2-2 draw kept Town in third place in the table.

There had been a two-month dalliance in the Full Members' Cup. A 2-1 win over Millwall back in December had preceded a perhaps more meaningful 4-1 home victory over First Division Norwich City toward the end of January.

Into the southern area semi-final, Town were defeated by a single goal by another top-flight side, Crystal Palace, in mid-February, so ending that potential route to Wembley. But coaches would still make the trip from Swindon to the twin towers before the season's end.

An Alan McLoughlin goal, the midfielder's 16th of the season, was enough to secure a point at Portsmouth in the last game of February, then a 3-0 home win over Port Vale cemented third place. The game brought a return for central defender Tim Parkin, who had departed for Vale Park in December.

It was also notable for an incredible goal from skipper Colin Calderwood. In the 11th minute the centre-back strolled up to take a free kick just inside the Vale half, shaped to drop it towards Shearer and White, and instead rattled the ball over the head of the visiting keeper.

The well-respected *Evening Advertiser*'s Clive King memorably commented, 'Vale keeper Mark Grew must have wished his name was "Grew Some More".'

White and Shearer, not to be upstaged by a defender, added a goal apiece before the break.

Another three goals did for Bradford City in a 3-1 win at the County Ground three days later. Again Shearer was on the mark, this time with a pair, the additional strike coming from midfielder Steve Foley. Ardiles's view was, 'We did not play too well but we still got the job done. The crowd now expect us to score three goals every game.'

As if in appeasement, Town then rounded off a hectic week with another three at Plymouth, and this time they also kept a clean sheet. Shearer scored his fourth in seven days but was upstaged by partner White, who grabbed two.

Undefeated in seven matches. Three wins on the trot during which nine goals were scored and just one conceded. Town had now occupied third place for seven weeks, but there was about to be another stutter in the push for promotion.

On 17 March ex-Swindon striker Dave Bamber came back to the County Ground with Hull. Back in November while with Stoke he'd put through his own net. This time he scored the 89th-minute clincher at the right end of the pitch, which meant the visitors left with all three points after a 3-1 win. Shearer was on the mark for the fourth consecutive game, but his effort was in vain.

Then Swindon lost by a single goal at Ipswich and followed that up with draws against Oxford and Leicester at the end of March. In themselves, not terrible results, and they retained third place, but was momentum deserting Ossie Ardiles's side?

Town showed their nerves by missing two penalties against Leicester, with Paul Bodin and Tom Jones both failing to complete from 12 yards. With eight games to go it would be a dangerous time to lose impetus.

In the denouement, while only two would be lost, only three would be won. With the Uniteds of Leeds and Sheffield looking safe for the top two places, would that be enough to retain a play-off spot?

A week into April, off-field matters again drew attention away from the promotion run-in. The FA announced that Brian Hillier's appeal against his six-month suspension from football had been rejected. Not only that, possibly as a deterrent to any other potential miscreant within football challenging the FA's authority, the ban was increased to three years, while Lou Macari's £1,000 fine had been upheld.

It was reported that the club, perhaps judging how ineffective appeals had been for Hillier and Macari, had withdrawn its own appeal against a £7,500 fine imposed by the FA.

It was suggested by one of the other club officials that Hillier had little choice but to abandon thoughts of returning to his role. Vice-chairman Gary Herbert was announced as Hillier's successor, while the Football League continued to deliberate its actions regarding the allegations that Town had made illicit payments to players. Not the best preparations for a football club to maintain a promotion push.

Surely realising that there was little that he could do regarding the situation, Ossie Ardiles largely, and wisely, remained silent. His job was to ensure his players remained fully committed to on-field activities and focused on the promotion push.

So, amid all the developing uncertainty, Jon Gittens scored a late goal at Bournemouth on 7 April to help clinch a 2-1 win on the south coast. His diving header supplemented a seventh-minute opener from Fitzroy Simpson.

But perhaps most attention was grabbed by debutant keeper Kevin Dearden, a late replacement for Fraser Digby who was suffering from an eye infection, leaving the 20-year-old Tottenham loanee just a couple of hours to prepare. Signed as cover while second choice Nicky Hammond was injured, he acquitted himself admirably in what was his first of just two appearances during his loan spell.

One of the ongoing characteristics of Town's season had been the ability to gain notable and creditable performances away from home, then let themselves down a week later back at the County Ground. So it came as little surprise that just three days after the win at Dean Court, fellow south coast club Brighton came to Wiltshire on a Tuesday night and departed with the points.

Digby, restored between the posts, was beaten less than ten minutes after the kick-off, and by the break the visitors led 2-0. Shearer was replaced by Shaun Close at half-time, and White volleyed a goal back ten minutes into the second period for his 23rd of the campaign. Despite pressing, Swindon couldn't find an equaliser, leaving coach Chic Bates, plainly angered by the performance, to proclaim, 'We lost the game in the first half. We just didn't close down or challenge at all.'

Six games to go and down to fourth in the table. A finish above seventh would be needed to qualify for the end-of-season play-off circus.

Back at the County Ground at the weekend, Watford were the visitors. Twelve points off the relegation places, but a similar number from the play-off zone, the Hornets appeared to have little to play for. Ardiles's programme notes stated, 'All our matches now will have a tremendous bearing on the eventual promotion and play-off places, with our away games at Blackburn and Newcastle being virtually six-pointers.'

And it was in this light that Shearer and White maintained their season-long rivalry to finish as Town's top scorer. Second-half goals from each respectively represented their 25th and 24th of the season. The introduction of midfielder Steve Foley off the bench on the hour with the game goalless was considered the turning point.

The industrious 'Stigger' had spent much of the season injured, but Ardiles knew how influential he could be: 'He's a very, very important part of our team. He was phenomenal. We need him, especially with five games to go. It's a big boost to have him back.'

A clean sheet meant a 2-0 victory and the promotion campaign continued; having talked up the importance of the forthcoming game against Blackburn, Ardiles took his team to Ewood Park on 16 April hoping to build on the Watford win.

However, any excessive optimism evaporated into the Easter Monday sky. Blackburn claimed a 2-1 success as Town produced a mistake-riddled performance which saw their hosts leapfrog them into fourth. Mark Atkins capitalised on a fumble by Digby to open the scoring in the first minute, then Jon Gittens gave the Robins a boost immediately before half-time with a brave headed equaliser.

But the reprieve lasted for less than 90 seconds after the restart as Simon Garner scored what would prove to be the winner.

The encounter, while not helping Town's promotion hopes, would prove to be significant before the end of May. Which side had learned most about the other?

The last victory of the regular season came at the County Ground when relegation-threatened West Bromwich Albion departed on the wrong end of a 2-1 scoreline. A forgettable goalless first half saw Swindon give a listless performance, but White's 81st-minute tap-in for his 25th goal of the season was enough to keep another three points in Wiltshire.

Shearer's work had set White up for the easy finish; 'Chalkie' commented, 'I couldn't really miss, could I? It was a case of being in the right place at the right time. The game was a bit scrappy, but games are bound to be tight at this time of the season.'

Paul Bodin had scored three minutes into the second period when his deflected free kick rolled into the opposition's net, and in between Don Goodman had equalised.

Sitting fifth in the table, there were just three more matches to play, and all three would be drawn.

The performance of Fraser Digby was mostly responsible for a 0-0 draw at St James' Park when Newcastle, who would eventually finish the campaign in third, failed to break down a resolute Swindon defence. Then Middlesbrough, battling against the drop to the Third Division, left the County Ground with a point three days later. Steve Foley had the distinction of scoring the goal that virtually booked Town's participation in the play-offs for the second consecutive season. His 50th-minute strike settled nerves after Bernie Slaven's 30th-minute opener.

There was a five-point gap between Sunderland in sixth and West Ham in seventh, with those finishing above the divide claiming a play-off spot, but as it turned out all four participants had now been decided. A last-day visit to Stoke on 5 May brought a goal for Shearer, a point for Town and the finish to the regular season.

Three teams now stood between Swindon and the First Division. Newcastle had finished the season in third on 80 points, while Swindon, Blackburn and Sunderland had finished fourth, fifth and sixth respectively. That trio were on 74 points, separated only by goal difference.

All would fight it out for promotion, and only one would be in the First Division the following season. The outcome should have been determined on a football pitch. It would be anything but.

On 1 May, the local press ran a story telling how police and tax officials had descended on a variety of addresses to arrest Brian Hillier, Lou Macari, former accountant Vince Farrar and Swindon captain Colin Calderwood. It was said that regional crime squad officers and members of the Inland Revenue had swooped in earlier that day, and that all four men were being held for allegedly conspiring to defraud the public purse. Calderwood was released without charge almost immediately.

The Football League, which was due to conduct a hearing regarding 36 charges of financial irregularities on 4 May, was preparing to postpone the event.

Meanwhile, Ardiles was left to try to prepare his team for a play-off campaign that was designed to determine the constitution of the following season's First Division; his team were due to face Blackburn at Ewood Park on 13 May in the first leg of the semi-final.

Only days earlier, Ardiles's programme notes had said, 'As you have probably noticed, I have remained silent through all the controversies. It was the only way, I believe, to shield the players from the enormous pressures that they have been under. All credit to them. They have responded to the challenges.'

Supporters may have felt further trepidation about a potential note of finality in Ossie's last statement, 'It has been a pleasure to work with them.'

On 3 May, Hillier, Macari and Farrar appeared in court charged with tax offences, and a trip to Villa Park where Town officials were due to appear before the Football League Management Committee was postponed in order that the commission could study further documentation about the case.

Ominously, the *Evening Advertiser* reminded readers that the league had powers to impose a range of punishments, from a points deduction to relegation.

On 13 May, everyone was relieved when football returned. Swindon at last had the chance to concentrate on their footballing superiority. It was an opportunity that was taken with a vengeance.

Beaten at Ewood Park less than a month earlier, Ossie's men showed that they had learned the lesson with a win that was more emphatic than the scoreline suggested. Outplaying their hosts with incisive passing, the 2-1 success was widely acclaimed by the suddenly attentive national press to have been a let-off for Blackburn.

David Kerslake's cross found White on the half-hour mark, and the striker's 26th goal of the season arrived when he turned on the edge of the penalty area to fire an immaculate shot just under the crossbar.

If that was spectacular, even it couldn't match the effort from Steve Foley, whose stunning volley after the ball had been cleared from a corner flashed past bemused Rovers keeper Terry Gennoe on 55 minutes to put daylight between the teams.

An uncharacteristic mistake from Ross MacLaren took some shine off the proceedings; the midfielder mis-controlled the ball and Andy Kennedy raced 30 yards to beat the advancing Digby. But the general consensus suggested that Town could have had six, and the tie was poised for an equally dramatic second leg at the County Ground three days later.

The two teams met again on Wednesday, 16 May, and the outcome was exactly the same.

Again White was on the scoresheet, this time accompanied by fellow frontman Shearer. Again Town took a two-goal lead, and again Rovers hit back, with what was by that point a consolation goal.

Shearer had started the fiesta in the 35th minute when he intercepted a loose pass between defender David Mail and Gennoe to curl a shot over the keeper, despite a desperate attempt by Chris Sulley to hook it off the line. Just three minutes later it was 2-0 when Shearer this time broke down the left, crossed towards goal, and White outsmarted the hapless Mail again to double the lead.

When Howard Gayle struck for the travelling team midway through the second half there was time for Blackburn to desperately press to get back into the game, but their efforts were to be in vain. Aggregate score: Swindon Town 4 Blackburn Rovers 2.

After the match, Ossie understated, 'You could say I'm extremely pleased. We'd done the hard part by winning at Blackburn and nerves meant we couldn't play our normal game, yet the response of the players was magnificent, and I have nothing but praise for them.'

Town had qualified for a Wembley final where they would meet Sunderland, and as determined before a ball had been kicked back in August, the winners were expected to gain promotion to the First Division.

Gordon Taylor, chief executive of the Professional Footballers' Association, had by now thrown his twopenn'orth into the off-field dramas, declaring, 'It would be an unfair penalty on the supporters of Swindon, along with the players if, in spite of the efforts of manager Ossie Ardiles, this was all to be thrown in their faces.'

Everyone with a love of Swindon Town Football Club agreed.

There were 12 days to prepare for the bank holiday date at Wembley, and most of the media concentrated on footballing preparations for the big day. Some felt that the closer it came, the greater the possibility that the harshest potential penalties from the footballing authorities had been avoided.

It would surely be inappropriate to allow Swindon to play a Wembley final and perhaps win promotion, only for the powers that be to take it away, some thought. If they were going to do that then they would have acted earlier, people reasoned. Wouldn't delaying the punishment look like weakness? Would allowing Town to play the game, knowing that the prize would be taken away, and all the lucrative income from the match collected by the football authorities, be at least unethical? Perhaps even fraudulent?

The morning of the bank holiday Monday arrived, and much of the population of Swindon and its surrounding areas were on the M4 or on the train on their way to Wembley. Altogether 33,000 tickets had been sold to Town supporters, who were to comprise 45 per cent of the 72,873 crowd.

Sunderland had opened the regular season with victory at the County Ground, while Swindon had recovered some kudos with a draw at Roker Park in December. Both teams had finished the campaign on 74 points, while a superior goal difference of 14 in Town's favour had left them two places higher in the table.

So there was little to choose between the teams, and the stage was set for an epic encounter. Whether that expectation was met would depend on how the red and white of the rivals' colours was configured – the solid red of Swindon or the stripes of the Rokermen.

In the event Sunderland switched to all blue, and it was the Wearsiders who made the bigger early impact. Marco Gabbiadini couldn't quite reach an Eric Gates cross, then Gates himself couldn't capitalise on an opportunity to take a clear shot at goal. Pressure continued as Colin Calderwood diverted an effort from Gabbiadini into the side netting. Then Town started to exert control.

Steve White shot over the bar after seven minutes, then he forced a diving save from Tony Norman after a Duncan Shearer header had brought about the opportunity. The impressive White then saw his shot roll against the post after he had intercepted a weak backpass, and Shearer was just unable to tuck away the rebound.

At times it seemed that only Norman was standing in the way of a Town goal and his knees just prevented Tom Jones from breaking the deadlock before the 5ft 7in Steve Foley headed just over the bar.

Then in the 26th minute came the decisive moment. Defender David Kerslake won the ball in the middle of the park and it ran towards Alan McLoughlin. Still some 30 yards out, McLoughlin advanced sufficiently to try his luck and hit a goal-bound shot that might have troubled Norman less than some of the other attempts he had already dealt with.

However, the ball struck defender Gary Bennett and looped over the already committed Norman into the back of the net.

The goal might have been scrappy, it might have been harsh on Bennett and Norman, but it was well deserved on the strength of the run of play, and Swindon supporters weren't about to give too much thought to the feelings of the opposing side.

Further opportunities came to White, Jones and McLoughlin to increase the lead, but half-time arrived with just the one goal separating the two sides. Would it be enough to see off the Rokermen?

Well, yes. The second half continued in much the same vein as the first; Shearer steered a chance just wide of the post, and a rare opportunity for Gary Owers was snuffed out by a combination of Ross MacLaren and Jon Gittens. Back at the Sunderland end, Norman and Bennett combined to prevent a double attempt from the dangerous White, and an effort from the ever-industrious Foley was denied by the overworked Bennett.

As the clock ran down, Norman's fingertips prevented Shearer from adding the second goal and bringing the hyperventilating supporters some relief, before referee John Martin blew for full time after three added minutes. Many who watched the spectacle believed it may have been the most one-sided 1-0 victory they had ever seen.

Colin Calderwood climbed the steps to collect the trophy, Town supporters continued to sing themselves hoarse and the Sunderland fans slumped in disbelief. There was one long party on the coaches and trains back to Wiltshire, followed by one long party in the Swindon district of Old Town.

After 70 years of Football League membership, and 111 after the club's foundation, Swindon had finally reached the top flight.

But over the hysteria of celebration there hung a dark shadow. The elephant in the room remained. What action would the authorities take regarding the financial irregularities investigation?

As the celebrations ran their course and the hangovers cleared, the mood began to change to one of trepidation. Ossie Ardiles was quoted as saying, 'I still hope that somehow the league will look at us sympathetically and help us if they like what they have seen. It would be a tragedy if we were denied now, from the players' and supporters' view. As time goes on, we are somehow more confident that we will be in the First Division next season.'

Was this hope, expectation or wishful thinking?

On 6 June, the Football League Management Committee convened at Villa Park for its delayed deliberations regarding 36 irregular payments to players. It had been over a week since Town had beaten Sunderland at Wembley and once the jubilations had subsided there had been little else on the minds of officials, players and supporters.

So finally, after a pregnant pause that seemed the length normally associated with the gestation period of the aforementioned elephant, a decision was to be made.

By the end of the day and after an eight-hour meeting, it was announced that Swindon would be relegated two divisions, from the First Division to which promotion had been so recently won, down to the third tier, while Sunderland would be promoted in their place.

Swindon had won the battle. Sunderland had won the prize.

There was outrage at the announcement. Steve White, so influential at Wembley, said, 'It has shattered our club. The decision seems so unfair. Why did they let us go to Wembley and win the play-offs if this is what they had in mind?'

Former manager Lou Macari remarked, 'Without a doubt this is very harsh. I am disgusted and feel very disappointed for the club and all the supporters.'

The word on everybody's lips was 'devastated'. Protest marches took place around the town and 300 fans staged a sit-in at the County Ground, all hoping to attract enough attention to force a reconsideration.

After an emergency meeting of the board, it was announced that an appeal to have the double demotion reversed would commence. Ardiles returned from holiday in Argentina and vowed to remain at the club and fans proclaimed that they had been tricked into parting with their money for a trip to Wembley, suspecting that the punishment had already been decided.

Colin Calderwood said, 'We are glad the club are appealing, and we pin our hopes that the football authorities impose a more appropriate and reasonable penalty.'

Town announced the decision to scrap the idea of appealing to the FA, and go directly to the High Court instead, but while the Court ruled that the law did have authority over the FA, the club backtracked and placed fresh efforts in convincing the FA to reconsider its original punishment.

The whole affair was convoluted, and there appeared to be a certain amount of posturing and bluff-calling going on. On 2 July, a three-man team from the FA reconvened to reconsider the double-relegation decision, and by the end of the day a fresh announcement was made: Swindon would now 'only' suffer relegation back to the Second Division, rather than down to the Third Division.

Reaction around Swindon was mixed. Some felt relief that Third Division football wouldn't be returning to the County Ground the following season, while fury still lingered that First Division clubs would not be the visitors.

But mostly there was relief that the whole affair had run its course, that Ardiles had announced he was committed to the club and that concentration could now be focused on replicating the footballing success of the previous 12 months.

All that was necessary now was to do it all again over the 1990/91 season.

2

1990/91

SWINDON TOWN'S 1990/91 season kicked off in the Second Division on 25 August, with everyone associated with the club still feeling raw and traumatised from the events at the tail end of the previous campaign.

There had been many sleepless nights, not quelled at all by England's appearance at the World Cup in Italy. For most committed club fans, watching their national team is a pale imitation of the feeling they get from supporting their club. That Bobby Robson led his team to a semi-final penalty shoot-out defeat was inconsequential in comparison to the drama that Swindon supporters had been through.

Town were facing another nine months of toil as they attempted to reproduce the performances of 1989/90. In the words of Alf Ramsey, the England World Cup-winning manager of 1966 as he prepared his team for extra time having seen victory snatched away in the 90th minute, 'You've won it once. Now go out and win it again.'

The previous summer, Ossie Ardiles had done little to change the squad he inherited from Lou Macari.

Similarly, the summer of 1990 was also conspicuous by the shortage of incoming players, but this time it was surely a result of the uncertainty that meant Ardiles didn't even know which division his side would compete in until 2 July, fewer than eight weeks before the start of 1990/91. How could anyone persuade a player to join a club which didn't know its status?

That left Ardiles playing catch-up as the kick-off approached. Many players who might have been considered legitimate transfer targets had understandably committed their future elsewhere by the time the boss could act.

But the quality of those who did arrive at the County Ground would demonstrate the influence that Ardiles had in the transfer market, and the inspiration such an international star could stimulate in prospective signings. The season was already six weeks old when an ex-Tottenham colleague, midfielder Micky Hazard, was persuaded to join from Portsmouth towards the end of September, and less than a month after that the squad was augmented by a player with a CV which trumped all who had come before him.

In Ossie Ardiles, Swindon were managed by someone who had won the World Cup 12 years earlier. Then the arrival of his fellow Argentinian, defender Néstor Lorenzo, from Italian club Bari in October raised the bar to unheard-of levels. Here was a man who had appeared in the World Cup Final just months earlier. His arrival was initially on a loan deal, but before the end of 1990 money changed hands and Lorenzo was a Swindon man. This looked like a real statement of intent to push for the promotion that had previously been denied.

But back to August, and Town kicked off the new season with a win at Charlton Athletic, newly relegated from Division One.

First-half goals from Paul Bodin and Duncan Shearer had opened the account with three points at The Valley, a therapeutic response to all that had happened earlier.

The close-season had been both fraught and short. Now that attention was back on the field of play, Swindon had delivered a statement which announced that they were back to winning ways. It said that the Second Division should watch out.

Ardiles said after the match, 'I am delighted with the result. We created a lot more chances than they did and although we gave them some openings, as long as we keep winning then there is no problem.'

So when Ipswich Town were despatched 1-0 at the County Ground three days later, Swindon had six points from six and sat level top in the embryonic table. Normal service had been resumed. The Robins seemed destined for another crack at promotion, Shearer was on the scoresheet again, this time on his 28th birthday, and all was right in the Swindon Town world.

It was by this point well known that Ardiles had his side playing with a midfield diamond, and Ipswich boss John Lyall had unsuccessfully attempted to counter the tactic by swamping the central area of the pitch to no avail. Almost 11,000 were present to see football return to the County Ground, with the Swindon performance more than worth the three-point haul.

The game against the Suffolk team offered the first chance for Ardiles to pass comment on the Wembley adventure and close-season events from the platform of the matchday programme, and he opened with skilful understatement, 'I think you could say that it's been an eventful summer!'

About the unrewarded triumph back in May, he said, 'I felt that the boys gave an outstanding performance, and we thoroughly deserved our victory. Sunderland must have found the 1-0 scoreline very flattering because we could easily have won by a much bigger margin. I would like to congratulate the supporters for their excellent behaviour. Not only did you contribute to an excellent Wembley atmosphere, but you also reacted positively to the Football League's decision to demote us to the Third Division.

'In my opinion the Football League's decision was extremely harsh, and although we did fight, through the High Court as well as through the FA and at least won back our place in the Second Division, I was still disappointed with the final outcome. Nevertheless, we must now put it to the back of our minds and try to win promotion again. It will be no formality. In fact, I expect it to be even more difficult than it was last season.'

So there was wringing of hands, holding of heads, but little surprise when it was announced on 4 September that the FA was investigating Swindon Town regarding further allegations of financial irregularities. Was this turning into a vendetta?

In the words of Talking Heads' 1980 song 'Once in a Lifetime', 'Same as it ever was.'

As everyone associated with Swindon thought 'here we go again', it was perhaps no shock that the early season momentum on the pitch was to stutter, and a 1-0 defeat at home to recently promoted Bristol City shattered any premature, and ultimately misplaced optimism.

Ardiles's programme notes made no mention of the FA's renewed interest in the club but said, 'We have got off to a marvellous start and newspaper reports are already talking about promotion, but it is foolish to talk about it too soon.'

More points were dropped with a defensive mix-up leading to a draw at Hull City. Colin Calderwood and

Jon Gittens each left a long ball to the other, then skipper Calderwood belatedly lunged in and only diverted it to City's Neil Buckley, who slotted under Fraser Digby. Alan McLoughlin had only just given Town the lead, with the defensive lapse costing two points.

Then a 3-1 loss at home to Middlesbrough continued the slump. Shearer opened the scoring with his third of the season – continuing his form having been the joint top scorer in 1989/90 – to give Swindon the lead at the break, but a Bernie Slaven double and one from Robbie Mustoe saw the points go to Teesside. The game was notable for Ardiles's decision to bring the young Adi Viveash on as a replacement for the injured McLoughlin, only to subsequently bring Nicky Summerbee on as a tactical replacement for the unlucky Viveash.

But the unusual pack-shuffling was all in vain. By the end of the afternoon, the culmination of the first five games of the season meant that Swindon had dropped to mid-table.

During the entire campaign Town were to win consecutive Second Division matches just three times, not the level of consistency likely to produce a top-of-the-table challenge. With the first of those doubles already recorded, and the league position heading in a downward direction, the next would come in handy.

And so it came to pass.

The visit of Wolverhampton Wanderers for a Tuesday night fixture brought a visit from the dangerous duo of England striker Steve Bull and his predatory partner, future Swindon forward Andy Mutch, but an uncharacteristic long-ball display from Town meant visiting keeper Mike Stowell had the busier night.

Shearer and Fitzroy Simpson both had chances from huge kicks from Digby, and the on-loan Maltese international John Buttigieg supplied the cross for another opportunity for Shearer.

Buttigieg had been hastily signed from Brentford days earlier to cover for the injured David Kerslake, just as long-term right-back David Hockaday departed for pastures new at Hull.

Buttigieg would make just two appearances in a Town shirt before returning to the Bees.

The decisive action came just after an hour, when Simpson supplied a cross from the right flank then collected the ball again as it ran loose from a goalmouth scramble to fire home from a tight angle. Calderwood was stretchered off with ligament damage after a tangle with Bull, an injury which would keep the talismanic skipper out of action for almost five months.

Before the night was through another player announced his intention to join Ardiles's triumphant team. Sheffield Wednesday winger Dave Bennett, an FA Cup winner with Coventry City in 1987, had been among the crowd at the County Ground, and post-match he declared his agreement to sign for a reported £60,000 fee. The move would prove to be one of huge disappointment and 'what might have been' for all parties.

In these pre-transfer window days, Ardiles appeared to be playing successful catch-up with his squad-building after the delayed start to his transfer activity.

Bennett made his debut at Oxford United the following Saturday; the game started at a furious pace, and could have ended in Town humiliation in what is always the keenest of derbies.

Just five minutes in, Oxford had been gifted a two-goal lead. From a corner David Penney blasted through a crowd of players as Town failed to clear the danger, then a Paul Simpson shot was spilled by Digby for Martin Foyle to knock into an empty net.

Fitzroy Simpson's 20-yard shot reduced the arrears then Steve Foley stabbed home the equaliser from close range on the stroke of half-time. So, when Shearer rounded off the recovery with a second-half brace, Swindon's embarrassing local capitulation had been thankfully avoided.

Two wins in four days. Could the consecutive victories herald a run back to the top and help reclaim the promotion that had been snatched away in June?

The visit of Millwall on the last day of September saw Lions striker Teddy Sheringham kept off the scoresheet in a goalless draw. Visiting boss Bruce Rioch was magnanimous in his post-match observations on Swindon, 'They are one of the best teams in the Football League, let alone the Second Division, and will beat a lot of teams here this season.'

Then a trip to table-topping Oldham Athletic featured the first match, first goal and first assist for new signing Micky Hazard. He opened the scoring after 24 minutes, and he supplied the defence-splitting pass for Bodin to add to the scoreline on 68.

But with the score standing at 2-2, a match-deciding incident saw referee Colin Trussell first award a goal for the home side after ignoring what seemed an obvious push on Digby, then appear to change his mind after consulting a linesman.

But relief for the visiting supporters turned to disbelief as Trussell gestured to the penalty spot for what was adjudged to be a handball by defender Nicky Tanner, recently signed on loan from Liverpool to cover for the injured Calderwood.

Neil Redfearn netted the spot kick to claim a 3-2 win for the home side on the artificial pitch at Boundary Park, leaving Swindon fifth in the table.

Hazard's move to Swindon had been completed two days before the end of September, when £130,000 prised the ex-Tottenham Hotspur midfielder from Portsmouth. The new man had little hesitation in teaming up with his old Spurs midfield team-mate Ardiles.

'He was the biggest influence on my career when we were at Tottenham and a big factor in my decision to come here,' Hazard told the local press. 'I got the feeling I was no longer wanted at Portsmouth. I'm 30 now and I would like to spend my last two or three seasons in the First Division and I believe I can do that with Swindon. I saw them play at Wembley and I was very impressed. I see no reason why I can't help them go up again. I love the way Swindon play their football. The style we played at Tottenham was very similar. Keeping the ball and passing through midfield.'

A very complimentary assessment of the transformation of playing style that Ardiles had brought to his side since replacing Macari.

The signing of Hazard represented the biggest fee that Town had paid since the £110,000 signing of David Kerslake from Queens Park Rangers back in the previous November.

Four days later they were away again, this time southbound to Sussex to face Brighton & Hove Albion at the Goldstone Ground. The match was not one that Fraser Digby would choose to remember.

McLoughlin had already capitalised on a loose ball from a parried Steve White shot to tap home the opener, but five minutes later Digby failed to claim a corner, gifting Steve Gatting an easy headed equaliser.

And the game was still only 13 minutes old when the normally reliable Digby allowed a ball to squirm from his grasp and over the line having appeared to have already collected it safely. And things didn't get any more comfortable for the ex-England under-21 custodian.

Minutes before the break, the unfortunate Digby conceded a free kick for taking more than four steps while holding the ball, a rule that was to be dropped for the following season. As a defensive wall was being constructed, Digby inexplicably dashed in front of it and was hopelessly trying to reclaim his position when the ball was fired home by John Byrne to increase the home side's half-time advantage to 3-1.

With the dangerous Shearer suffering a hamstring strain and being replaced by the somewhat less effective Shaun Close, a second-half recovery looked a tall order.

But chances fell to Simpson and McLoughlin, and in the 56th minute a flowing move involving McLoughlin, White and Hazard resulted in a corner, from which a Gittens finish was disallowed for an offside decision given against Hazard.

With less than a quarter of an hour remaining Town's pressure finally told when McLoughlin calmly rounded Perry Digweed in the Seagulls goal to reduce the arrears, and the fightback was completed when White grabbed the equaliser after Digweed failed to hold a Simpson shot.

Even then there were chances for Town to win the encounter with Ross MacLaren testing Digweed from 20 yards and White having an effort ruled out for offside. After the Robins had been more successful conquering a rain-soaked pitch in blustery conditions than the home side, the points were shared.

Ten games into the season the high-scoring draw left Swindon tenth in the Second Division. While the point was welcome, returns would have to improve if Ardiles's side were to bring about the much hoped for response to the previous season's promotion denial.

Afterwards there was a disclosure of mitigating circumstances for Digby. 'He did extremely well to play today because he was injured,' revealed Ardiles. 'It showed his character because many others would have said play someone else. I am delighted with his contribution.' The boss went on to say, 'My boys have a very good attitude which they showed today. We never say die and always play for 90 minutes, but I think a draw was a fair result.'

Ardiles also went on to praise the growing midfield understanding between McLoughlin and Hazard, which was already showing encouraging signs as the season progressed into its third month.

In the second round of the League Cup in late September, Town travelled to Darlington, the team fated to claim the Fourth Division title at the end of the campaign.

Some observers may have considered the tie to have been over and done with. The first leg at Feethams resulted in a convincing 3-0 victory for the home side, and even with home advantage and holding a superior footballing status of two divisions, Swindon would do well to overturn that deficit.

Nevertheless, that was what would take place. Back in Wiltshire, Nicky Hammond replaced the injured Digby in goal for his first start in two and a half years, and Adi Viveash claimed his first start in defence. Goals from

Simpson and McLoughlin sandwiched an unfortunate own goal by Quakers defender Kevin Smith and a collector's item of a strike by Shaun Close: Swindon Town 4 Darlington 3 on aggregate.

Close had been signed by Ardiles a year earlier and over a four-season spell at the County Ground he would make 15 starts and add a further 38 appearances from the bench, scoring just twice. This was the first. When he departed for Barnet in August 1993, there were some supporters who felt justified in wondering whether Close's first name was Noteven, but this was his night.

While the evening ended in progression to round three for Town, over the two legs the tie was most notable for the devastating injury to Dave Bennett at Feethams. A double fracture of the right leg meant that he had signed, made his debut and played his last game for Town all in little over a week.

Bennett was to spend over a year battling back to fitness, only to suffer a repeat injury during a loan spell at Shrewsbury, a move which was designed to complete his rehabilitation. When he finally departed for non-league action in March 1994, he had sadly never taken to the County Ground pitch.

When the fixture list had been released there were two familiar West Country names added following their promotions from the Third Division. Town had already played, and lost to Bristol City in September, and in mid-October it was the turn of Rovers to visit the County Ground.

Without a league win in the last three attempts, victory against a local rival would bring a welcome fillip to a season which was perhaps beginning to flag.

This was surely the right time to re-stamp Town's credentials for a new promotion push. After Bristol City's County Ground victory no one in Swindon wished to relinquish points to a Bristol side twice in six weeks.

Of course, wishes don't always reap rewards.

'We were disgraceful,' said skipper Ross MacLaren after the match. 'Rovers completely outplayed us in every department. They raised their game. We did not. They showed all the fight and determination and the will to win.'

Tony Pounder, Rovers' summer signing from non-league Weymouth, did the early damage with his first league goal in the 33rd minute, then ten minutes from the end of the match Pounder was brought down by Hammond, resulting in future Robins boss Ian Holloway dispatching the spot kick to seal the match with a 2-0 win for the Gas.

Local pride had taken another battering. Was the season beginning to slip through Swindon's fingers?

A week later they were at home again. This time West Ham United travelled from the capital with the scoreline again reflecting poorly on Town's aspirations.

Despite an improved showing, a single goal from Frank McAvennie eight minutes from time did for Town in front of an attendance of over 13,500. McAvennie, who would spend a three-month loan from Celtic at the County Ground in 1994, had replaced ex-Town favourite Jim Quinn with 20 minutes to go.

The result left Ardiles's team 11th in the table and slipping downwards. Meanwhile, unbeaten West Ham were on course for promotion back to the First Division.

Despite the return of Fraser Digby, an increasing injury list now included new loan signing Néstor Lorenzo (who had broken a toe in a reserve team match without making his first-team debut), Alan McLoughlin and Micky Hazard, added to the already suffering Shearer, Calderwood and long-term absentee Bennett. As Ardiles commented on the injury situation, 'It never rains unless it pours.'

With just two points to show from the previous five matches, a midweek trip to Leicester City as the last week of October commenced didn't offer great cause for optimism. Filbert Street had not been a happy hunting ground for Town over recent seasons, with dismissals contributing to reducing their points haul on multiple occasions.

So when David Kerslake mistimed a tackle on the halfway line, no one who travelled from Swindon would have been in the least surprised when referee John Kirkby produced a red card. The game was just three minutes old and Kerslake had been dismissed for the first time in his career.

Midfielder Tom Jones dropped to right-back to fill the defensive void, and City began an attacking onslaught designed to capitalise on their numerical superiority. But showing stoic resolution, it was Shearer who opened the scoring on his return from injury. His 24th-minute header finished a flowing move which saw Bodin and Simpson combine, culminating in a pinpoint cross which fell invitingly for Town's leading scorer to finish.

White then saw an effort strike a post and deflect to safety, then five minutes after the break he intercepted a backpass, rounded the City keeper and doubled the lead for the ten men.

Swindon were showing the flourish that had been absent for much of the season as White had another goal-bound attempt headed off the line but inevitably, with the home crowd's vocal contribution becoming increasingly scathing towards their men, Leicester skipper Ally Mauchlen struck a 20-yarder which left Digby helpless. And in keeping with referees' contributions in previous trips to Filbert Street, Kirkby contrived to allow sufficient additional time for Paul Reid to dispatch the ball past Digby from 25 yards to conclude a 2-2 draw.

Surely a creditable point in the face of adversity could be used as a springboard for a turnaround in fortunes? Sadly, it wasn't.

Three days later a trip to Oakwell to take on Barnsley saw Town reduced to ten men again. This time the referee was Trevor West, but the outcome was the same as the previous Wednesday. The man in black showed a mystified Jon Gittens a red card in the 55th minute after the central defender appeared to have executed a perfectly legitimate dispossession of Andy Saville.

By then Town had already fallen a goal behind in the first half when Digby was unable to hold a slippery shot as it skidded off a rain-soaked pitch, leaving a loose ball which was tucked away.

But if that left a familiar feeling of being hard done by, it was compounded five minutes after the dismissal of Gittens when Saville took a theatrical tumble inside the box and West pointed to the spot. Steve Agnew converted and Town were left two goals behind, a man down and with over half an hour to play.

White netted to make the score 2-1, but the Tykes ran riot to end the game with a 5-1 win.

It's rarely necessary to scratch too far below the surface of any club to find a seam of perceived injustice, and after the authorities' dealings with Swindon in the summer, no one would have been surprised to detect a feeling of paranoia and perhaps conspiracy around the County Ground.

After the match the very personable Town assistant manager Chic Bates was moved to say, 'It is very disappointing. He has sent Jon Gittens off for a professional foul – if he calls that a professional foul he should be refereeing rugby league games. It just makes you wonder if the truth is known – have the league got it in for Swindon this season? These comments could get me into trouble but when you get decisions like we have had, something has to be said.'

The similarly mild-mannered Ardiles commented, 'I have my doubts if it was even a foul – it was certainly not a sending-off offence. We are one of the least physical teams in the Second Division but suddenly we are getting a lot of players sent off. And the penalty awarded against us was another example. It was a very controversial one.'

No such elucidations were offered a week later when Port Vale visited the County Ground and left with all three points after a 2-1 victory. A Swindon lead was courtesy of a Darren Beckford own goal after half an hour, and their performance was a lacklustre affair.

Swindon had gone eight games without a win, dropping to 18th in the table. The relegation places were suddenly looking too close for comfort.

Either side of the Port Vale loss the Robins had taken on the Owls of Sheffield Wednesday in the League Cup. A stout performance at Hillsborough on Halloween brought some scares from a home onslaught, and almost the treat of a last-gasp winner from Shearer, whose first-time volley produced an outstanding save from Wednesday keeper Kevin Pressman.

With the goalless outcome and honours even, a replay at the County Ground a week later brought a return to reality.

The only goal of the match came for Wednesday in the tenth minute, and they progressed into the fourth round. This time Pressman was not called into meaningful action for the entire 90 minutes, and despite the turgid display from his side Ardiles tried to be upbeat: 'We are not playing at our best right now, but it will come. It will be up to us to put it right.'

Steve White offered, 'Our confidence has taken a knock because we have only scored a few times at home.' The striker was not wrong. The last goal to be scored at the County Ground by a Swindon player had been in mid-September, six hours of playing time previously.

On 10 November it was the turn of Portsmouth to visit Wiltshire and there was good news on the injury front. With Liverpool loanee Nicky Tanner returning to his parent club, Ardiles was able to introduce Néstor Lorenzo to the centre of defence, as Gittens and Kerslake served suspensions.

Lorenzo's pedigree was not in doubt, and it took less than half an hour for him to make his mark in a Swindon shirt in what was his first competitive match since he appeared in the World Cup Final the previous July.

Calm and composed at the back, he was already proving a much-needed stabilising influence when he latched on to a Tom Jones cross to provide a powerful downward header to open the scoring on 29 minutes. The goal finally ended a 419-minute wait for a Robins player to score at the County Ground.

Perhaps with a weight off their shoulders, Shearer and White both had chances to increase the lead, before the two combined five minutes ahead of the break, allowing the ball to run loose to Steve Foley. The midfielder buried the opportunity and like London buses, Town had two goals after waiting so long for one.

Pompey were reduced to ten men when Martin Kuhl was sent off for a foul on Fitzroy Simpson, and the afternoon was rounded off when Adi Viveash, perhaps inspired by the coolness of his defensive partner Lorenzo, strode confidently forward and found a perfect pass to White. The striker then rounded the keeper before supplying a selfless cross for Shearer to nod home.

At last, a win, three goals, a clean sheet and a new hero. And no complaints about the referee. Just what was needed to kick-start the campaign.

A week later it was business as usual. For the second time in 11 days, Swindon faced Sheffield Wednesday and again tasted defeat. Then four consecutive draws stalled any hope of moving up a tightly compressed Second Division table. The Robins had recorded just one league win in 14 attempts.

The last of the draws, 1-1 at home to Charlton Athletic, saw Town booed off the pitch at half-time and led Ardiles to say, 'I have never seen a Swindon Town side play that badly. It was embarrassing. Defensively we did not do anything in the first half – we were always second best, and simply not good enough in attack.'

After 20 games Town stood 15th in a condensed division which saw just seven points separate seventh-placed Notts County and third-bottom Portsmouth.

It was a week until Christmas and just a couple of wins could propel Town towards the play-offs, but those three-point hauls were remaining incredibly elusive and with every passing week the top end of the table was becoming more remote.

Swindon had travelled to Stamford Bridge on 12 December in the Full Members' Cup, a tournament becoming increasingly obscure. Chelsea 'gloried' as holders of the trophy, and a functional 1-0 win for the London side took them through to the next round.

From Swindon's point of view the game was notable for the performance of Fraser Digby, who had announced his intention to sign a new contract a couple of weeks earlier. The 23-year-old had been linked with moves to West Ham and Aberdeen and his contentment in remaining was a boost for Ardiles.

Digby said, 'To be honest I don't read a lot of newspapers so as far as I'm concerned speculation means nothing to me. My future at the moment is with Swindon Town and I hope we can climb up the league. Ossie has been to me with a new contract, but the details are not sorted yet. I've had a few good games and clearly people's names are linked here, there and everywhere, but I haven't thought about it. Apart from our league position, everything at Swindon is OK.'

He had been signed from Manchester United by Lou Macari for £30,000 in 1986 and had been virtually ever-present in the first team ever since, also winning England under-21 caps. He had become an intrinsic part of the club and been instrumental in all the success that had begun under Macari.

If Digby were to perform at a higher level, everyone around the club hoped it would come while wearing a Town shirt, and it was only fair to assume that his remaining at the County Ground would be dependent on the team's continued progression. If Swindon moved towards the wrong end of the table, that could only be detrimental to satisfying any player's ambitions.

And as if to demonstrate the tenuous nature of squad-building, two pieces of business were conducted in the weeks leading up to Christmas, with the completion of one facilitating the conclusion of the other.

On 13 December, Republic of Ireland international midfielder Alan McLoughlin moved on to Southampton for a figure accepted to be in the region of £1m when all add-ons were accounted for. He had been with the club for five seasons and had grown from someone who seemed destined to be a right-sided defender into a predatory goalscorer at the head of Ardiles's midfield diamond, with an industrious work rate and eye for goal that made him a natural for the role. His five goals made him the club's second-top scorer at the time of his departure.

McLoughlin's goal at Wembley had looked like being the one to take Swindon to the First Division before the football authorities stepped in, but this move would take him to that level – albeit without the club.

The incoming fee would justify the reported £400,000 required to formalise the permanent signing of Néstor Lorenzo from Bari, and while that seemed welcome business, everyone who had watched McLoughlin develop would have been sorely disappointed that the two had featured together on just four occasions.

Lorenzo's matchday availability had previously been impinged by a work permit issue, but the signing of a permanent contract would circumvent such problems.

Headlines containing such sums in connection with Swindon Town were previously unheard of. The previous record incoming transfer fee had been £400,000 for the sale of left-back Phil King to Sheffield Wednesday 12 months previously, the record expenditure £250,000 to Huddersfield Town for Duncan Shearer in June 1988.

Hopes were that the undoubted strengthening of the defence with the arrival of Lorenzo would compensate for the loss of the attacking contribution of the departing McLoughlin, but as with all transfers there was an undeniable and unavoidable gamble.

And as always of course, Swindon were in need of the positive cash flow.

Just as the festive period loomed, a story emerged that scratched wounds which had barely begun to heal at the County Ground. Exeter City, Fourth Division champions the previous season, had been fined for financial misconduct involving grants from the Football Grounds Improvement Trust, the club's financial director had been banned for six months, and other fines had been issued – but there had been no relegation for the newly promoted side.

'Does the FA have double standards?' asked the *Evening Advertiser.*

And as if to prove that good news travels slower than bad, three days before New Year's Eve, glacially paced FA mechanisms announced that Swindon were no longer to be subject to potential charges from the investigation regarding alleged financial irregularities, begun at the beginning of September.

Predictably, the announcement went almost unnoticed in the media.

Three days ahead of Christmas though, in the programme for the County Ground match against West Bromwich Albion, Ardiles appraised his tenure so far: 'This season's form has been very disappointing and the main reason for this is the events of last summer. This has upset the lads more than they like to say and has shown in a lack of confidence. My confidence remains unscathed. All the players have been simply superb in showing their confidence in me and I would like to thank them 100 per cent. We do have problems right now, but it is no good feeling sorry for ourselves. My 18 months in charge have been very exciting and I am sure a lot more excitement is on the way.'

Goals from MacLaren and Shearer in three second-half minutes overturned a one-goal deficit to bring a first victory in six weeks. It was an early Christmas present, the glow from which would need to last considerably longer than the leftover turkey as the impasses resumed.

Because a goal apiece at Newcastle and a 2-2 draw at Watford was followed by a 1-1 stalemate at home to Plymouth Argyle on New Year's Day courtesy of Steve Foley's 90th-minute equaliser, Swindon remained steadfastly in mid-table, equidistant from the play-off and relegation places.

A little over halfway through the season and things could swing either way. Turn draws into wins, and a promotion place challenge was still possible. Let them slip into defeats and relegation was a distinct danger.

News that Colin Calderwood's recovery after tearing two knee ligaments was progressing well was a major boost. The thought of the cultured Calderwood alongside the classy Néstor Lorenzo in defence was a lip-smacking prospect.

Time, then, for more reason for dissatisfaction and feelings of injustice.

'GUILTY!' shouted the national headlines. 'CHELSEA HIT BY RECORD FINE'. It was reported that the Stamford Bridge club had been found guilty by a three-man league commission of irregular payments to players and the Blues had been handed a fine of £105,000, a figure which was reckoned to be equivalent to one Saturday's match receipts.

Chairman Ken Bates was reported to have pleaded his innocence but had offered no evidence to support his position. Bates, incredibly a serving member of the Football League Management Committee, was quoted as saying that he had no intention of resigning from his role and was said to feel the punishment was 'vindictive and excessive', while Swindon MP Simon Coombes described the outcome as 'a slap on the wrist' compared to the punishment previously handed out to the Robins.

The general feeling around the town was that there was 'one law for the big clubs, and another for the smaller ones', a particularly relevant point when a national newspaper claimed that Chelsea's magnitude of alleged irregular payments outstripped that made by Swindon.

Further astonishment was voiced that the whole issue had gone unreported until the verdict had been announced, while Swindon's case had been newspaper fodder for months, with the club tried, convicted and sentenced by the media before the outcome was decided.

And the furore was not confined to the streets of Swindon. Exeter City's secretary was quoted as saying, 'It stinks. It's a cover-up.' Sensibly, Town maintained a strictly 'no comment' position.

But back to pitch-based matters. As the story rumbled on and 1991 approached the middle of its first month, Swindon travelled to Ashton Gate to face Bristol City in the first away league match of the new year.

The indignation generated by events at Chelsea ran the risk of misdirecting focus away from the need to improve performances and results. With the loss of face that had already been inflicted in defeats by both Bristol clubs, the need for a good result was paramount.

Come five o'clock on 12 January there was real relief, and a belief that 1991 could improve on Swindon's mid-table stagnation. Ex-Bristol Rovers striker Steve White had ended a three-month goal drought with a brace that, when added to strikes from Micky Hazard and Duncan Shearer sandwiched between his efforts, plus the clean sheet kept by Fraser Digby, meant Town travelled eastwards back along the M4 with a 4-0 victory and three very welcome points in the bag.

A week later, bottom-of-the-table Hull City made the long haul to Wiltshire and departed on the end of a 3-1 loss. Again, White was on the scoresheet, this time with Shearer adding a pair. It was only the third time that Town had won two games on the trot that season. And worryingly, it was the last.

January had begun with FA Cup third round action against Third Division Leyton Orient, Shearer opening the scoring at Brisbane Road with his 12th of the season in the fifth minute. If that was expected to calm nerves of an upset, Orient had other ideas, pressing Town all the way and equalising with five minutes remaining to take the tie back to the County Ground.

But on 8 January, that presented a problem which it seemed only the Robins' home was subject to, and it would turn into quite a saga.

The ancient Shrivenham Road Stand was second-hand when it was rebuilt in 1958. It had previously seen service at the Aldershot military tattoo ground, where best guesses suggest it had already stood for around 30 years. Its twin sister had made its way to Peel Park, Accrington.

The corrugated iron structure was deemed unsafe in winds above gale force eight, so when the Bristol Weather Centre advised of gusts potentially touching force ten, to stage the replay would have been contrary to the ground's safety certificate, so forcing a postponement.

Six days later, on a very cold but still Monday night, the replay kicked off at the second attempt after a pitch inspection by referee Mike Bailey, who deemed, while safe and playable, that it was close to frozen. By half-time the thermometer had dropped from -1°C to -4°C. After Paul Bodin had put Town ahead, and the O's had equalised just a minute later, the game was abandoned on 54 minutes.

A week after that, the ground was still in such a state of permafrost that postponement again proved inevitable. Once again the Shrivenham Road Stand was mostly to blame as, just as for decades, its shadow kept that side of the pitch in shade, preventing a thaw.

Finally, on 21 January, the replay kicked off (again) and it took 89 minutes before White scored the only goal of the match, at last deciding the encounter in Swindon's favour.

The prize was a fourth-round tie at First Division Norwich City, which was to end Swindon's FA Cup participation for the season. But the story at Carrow Road was also far from straightforward as Town were to spend over half an hour with only nine men.

Central defender partners Néstor Lorenzo and Jon Gittens were both shown red cards, Lorenzo being dismissed in the 24th minute for pulling down a goal-bound Robert Fleck. When Gittens followed him into the bath in the 55th after retaliating to a late Fleck challenge, against the odds Swindon already held a one-goal lead, White having netted a 50th-minute opener for the, at that stage, ten-man visitors. Unsurprisingly, with the further red card the Canaries' superior headcount proved irresistible, with three goals taking the Norfolk side through to round four.

The dismissals left Lorenzo and Gittens in danger of three-match bans, not something that could be considered ideal with Colin Calderwood still some weeks away from returning from injury. Pending the confirmation of the suspensions, youngster Adi Viveash was the only available recognised centre-back at the club.

A 2-0 defeat at fifth-placed Middlesbrough as February started brought frustration for Ardiles, 'I felt it was a game we lost rather than one that they won. We made some errors that we shouldn't have done at the back and got punished. It was a close game between two evenly balanced teams but unfortunately, we made the crucial mistakes and that was the difference. We finished the game strongly, but their goalkeeper had an excellent game.'

Two goals inside four pre-break minutes gave the Ayresome Park team the win.

If momentum had increasingly stalled for Ardiles's side, Middlesbrough's future Swindon boss Colin Todd was complimentary towards the Wiltshire visitors. Pleased that his side had taken all six points off Town, he said, 'Swindon are a wonderful team to watch, and I still think they will make the play-offs. And after what happened to them last year, I think they deserve to be there.'

And continuing a managerial theme, with Lou Macari appointed manager of Birmingham City on 7 February, expectations were growing that Swindon's assistant Chic Bates was set to join him. As the season slipped through Town's fingers and Ardiles appeared to demonstrate increasing frustration, just how significant would the loss of his number two be?

Extreme cold weather was still gripping the country, and as a result of the impact on the fixture list it would be some time before the consequences would be felt. Bates vacated the County Ground for St Andrew's as expected, and Ardiles moved to appoint Tony Galvin as his new number two. Galvin had not made a first-team start since November 1989, and as an ex-Tottenham Hotspur team-mate of Ardiles he was a well-known and trusted colleague.

Galvin was also immediately available and could be appointed without a fee changing hands. That, as it was to be proved, would be quite beneficial.

Promotion-seeking Sheffield Wednesday arrived at the frost-free County Ground on Tuesday, 19 February. The weather-enforced break had given Colin Calderwood the necessary time to complete his recovery and he was named on the bench after a five-month absence. Viveash and MacLaren remained at the centre of defence with Lorenzo and Gittens mid-suspension, and 20-year-old midfielder Fitzroy Simpson made his first start of 1991.

The match was goalless at half-time and remained so until 15 minutes from the end. Then Simpson embarked on a run which took him past three defenders and placed an exquisite left-footed chip from 20 yards past keeper Chris Turner. Five minutes later David Hirst levelled for the visitors but eight minutes from time it was Simpson again who supplied the cross for Steve Foley to slam home the winner.

With a makeshift defence and with the assistant manager replaced, Swindon had risen to 11th in the table by defeating the team who occupied third. So three wins in the last four league games – perhaps *now* things could continue in a positive manner.

Calderwood was on the cusp of a return and Lorenzo and Gittens would be back from suspension. Could things still take a turn for the better? The break meant there were still 17 games to play; Swindon were 13 points off a play-off place and 13 points off relegation. Which direction would their season still turn?

In truth there had been the suggestions of new dawns before, and all had proved to be false. There were two and a half months of the season to run and this was to prove no exception. The much-desired repeat of their 1989/90 success was to remain elusive and there was more upheaval lurking over the horizon.

Defeat at a blustery Portsmouth was blamed on a defensive experiment by Ardiles which surrendered two goals inside five first-half minutes, and just five minutes after Steve White had given Town the lead. 'I don't particularly like playing an offside game, but with the problems we have in defence I decided to try it here,' explained Ardiles as he accepted blame for the defeat. 'Unfortunately, it did not work very well.'

Still without Lorenzo and Gittens, even the appearance of Calderwood off the bench failed to lift the team. New assistant boss Tony Galvin added, 'We started lethargically and apart from the front two [White and Shearer] who worked hard throughout, we had very little to offer. I thought the result flattered us.'

Two days into March, a trip to Blackburn Rovers brought Groundhog Day. Again White scored, this time to equalise a Simon Garner opener, but a Foley own goal gifted the home side the three points. Like Portsmouth before them, Rovers were in the bottom five and the result of each game dropped Swindon closer to joining them in a relegation battle.

But the defeat at Ewood Park was about to be overshadowed by the news that defender Paul Bodin was on his way out of the County Ground.

'There has been some interest from Crystal Palace, and we are talking to them,' said a dispirited Ardiles. 'I am in a position where I have to sell before I can buy any players so we will just have to see what happens between now and the transfer deadline day [28 March].'

Bodin, meanwhile, seemed in the dark, 'Ossie has not said anything to me, so I really don't know a lot about it. All I have heard about Crystal Palace is what has been reported in the newspapers.'

The 26-year-old, ever present that season, had been withdrawn at half-time at Blackburn, an action which had exacerbated the fragility of the rearguard.

Palace were reported to have made a bid which was close to Swindon's valuation, and if accepted, the loss of the Welsh international would further weaken an already suspect defence.

By the time Town took on Oxford at the County Ground on 5 March, Ardiles had resigned himself to losing the left-back, 'We are still talking to Crystal Palace and are quite close to reaching an agreement. It looks to me as though we are having to sell our best players and that is not good. The problem is that we just don't have any money to spend.'

And after witnessing a goalless stalemate, even the boss's post-match statement had an air of desperation, 'We are not going to get into the play-offs if we continue as we are playing at the moment, but if we can just put a good run together, we still have a chance.'

The programme cover showing Ardiles, Galvin and Micky Hazard wearing Comic Relief red noses tried in vain to lighten the mood. Perhaps the long nose of Pinocchio might have been more appropriate.

Within a day or two it was revealed that Palace had splashed out £550,000 to capture Bodin's signature. Clauses that could add extra sums after specific appearances would never come to fruition.

Bodin, while looking forward to testing himself in the First Division, was plainly very reluctant to leave the club. Realistically he accepted that Town were still paying the financial cost of enforced relegation in the summer.

The mood at the County Ground continued to turn sour as Ardiles expressed his dissatisfaction in the *Evening Advertiser.* While restating his ambition to manage Swindon in the First Division, the Argentinian was beginning to show his lack of conviction that the club could facilitate his aims.

Revealing that the fee to sign Néstor Lorenzo had actually been £160,000, rather than the reported £400,000, Ardiles demonstrated his frustration that so little of the incoming cash from the sale of Alan McLoughlin had been available for team rebuilding, indicating his expectations of a similar outcome regarding the inward-bound fee from the sale of Bodin: 'Since I have been here, we have made more than £2m on transfers, but spent little more than £500,000. I somehow feel that I am working for the bank manager rather than the football club.'

In response, chairman Ken Chapman released a statement quantifying the £1m loss from demotion and a further £250,000 in demands made by the FA and Inland Revenue. But the air was turning distinctly fetid.

Two more dropped home points in a 2-2 draw with Oldham didn't help, then a sequence of three consecutive losses saw Town slip to within five points of the relegation zone.

The hope that defeats could be turned into draws, and that draws could be turned into wins was proving nothing more than a pipe dream. Instead the inverse was happening, and March was about to deal more adverse circumstances.

Newcastle United manager Jim Smith announced his resignation as the month drew towards its close, and newspaper speculation put Ardiles at the top of the St James' Park wanted list.

Chapman said, 'There has been no approach, and if they did want to talk to our manager, they would have to come through me because he is under contract.' With Ardiles having signed an extended deal in the summer, there would be substantial compensation due. The man himself said, 'I do not know anything about it – it is just speculation.'

Supporters raised their eyebrows. The prospect of incoming money for the club surely meant this was a done deal. And Newcastle were due at the County Ground on 30 March.

Three days before transfer deadline day, Jon Gittens was sold to Southampton; the fee was reported to be £400,000. Two days later, Newcastle visited the County Ground and were duly despatched 3-2, and on April Fool's Day the newspapers announced that Ardiles had left for Tyneside.

'To be fair I had already made it known that I was going to leave soon – in the summer. The selling of players played a big part in my decision,' he explained.

Chapman revealed that he had been approached immediately after the defeat of the Magpies, leading to Ardiles talking to the visiting side's chairman George Forbes.

Just as all fans had guessed, the manager who had taken their side to Wembley victory, with the prize of top-flight football having been cruelly snatched away immediately after, was gone.

As is traditional, assistant boss Tony Galvin was installed as caretaker manager, and with equal predictability he swiftly announced his intended departure for St James' Park to follow his mentor.

Perhaps somewhat presumptuously Galvin, who had signed as a player 18 months previously, made just six starts and had acted as assistant manager for less than two months before announcing his exit, felt able to make his own recommendation of who should replace Ardiles.

'Give Hoddle the Town job says Galvin' proclaimed the *Evening Advertiser*. Jobs for the ex-Spurs boys it may have seemed, but no one would have argued against the sentiment towards Glenn Hoddle, the stylish former England international midfielder.

Swindon travelled to West Bromwich Albion and lost 2-1, and it had gone almost unnoticed that their scorer that day was Paul Rideout, the star striker of the early 1980s who had returned on loan from Southampton just as everything at the County Ground turned to turmoil.

But leading scorer Duncan Shearer was in agreement with Galvin, saying, 'Glenn's a big name, in fact they don't come much bigger, and if we can get him, it would be a tremendous boost for everybody. He is the same style of player as Ossie.' But succinctly, he added, 'One of the first questions will be whether there will be any money to spend on players.'

Colin Calderwood was sad to see Ardiles leave, 'I rate him very highly as a manager. He treated us all like adults and the way he gained respect was by giving us respect. That came from a man who has done everything in football.' Steve White agreed, 'We all thought the world of Ossie. He was very well liked.'

Meanwhile, Glenn Hoddle emerged as the club's first choice as well, and on 3 April discussions with the 33-year-old were progressing swiftly.

He had been released by Monaco the previous December as a serious knee injury threatened to curtail his playing career. Training with Chelsea, Hoddle was on the verge of recovering fitness and ready to revive his on-pitch activities, recently playing for the Londoners' reserves in his first outing in 20 months.

Through being registered with Chelsea and with the transfer deadline passed, it meant that if appointed, Hoddle would be unable to take to the pitch in a Swindon shirt until the start of 1991/92. Come the end of the day it seemed that most people's wishes had been fulfilled as Hoddle agreed a three-year contract as manager, installing John Gorman as his second in command.

'I am going to continue to try to resurrect my career and if by the beginning of next season I have regained the fitness and standard required, then by all means I will become a player-manager. I will be keeping the good things that Ossie left and be adding the things that John and I are working towards. Ultimately, we want promotion for Swindon Town,' Hoddle admitted.

But first, with eight games and six weeks of the season left, there was an alarming plummet down the table to arrest, starting with a home match against Watford.

'I'm pleased to have been able to come to Swindon,' Hoddle's programme notes proclaimed. 'I know of the problems and disappointments the club has had in the past, but we now have to look to the future.'

No one in Swindon would disagree. Too much retrospective angst had been expended since demotion had robbed everyone of their top-flight destiny, and the authorities' desire to see Swindon in the Third Division was too close to coming to fruition for comfort. Before concentrating on the longer term, there was still a job to do before the end of 1990/91.

A 2-1 defeat at the hands of the Hornets didn't help with those preliminary aims. Hoddle's initial assessment was, 'We looked a very accomplished side at times, but there is a lot of work to do on the training ground, mainly defensively. We played some lovely football for half an hour and then let them score.'

A week later Hoddle's new side travelled to Devon to take on Plymouth Argyle. An unfortunate mistake nine minutes from time while Town led 3-2 saw Adi Viveash, settling in at left-back since the departure of Bodin, guide a routine pass back to Fraser Digby only to find the goalkeeper was not where the defender thought he'd be.

The faux pas gifted the home side an equaliser and a point, a result that even Argyle boss David Kemp thought was unjustified, 'I felt very sorry for Swindon. They attacked for 90 minutes yet we got a point we certainly did not deserve.'

Hoddle said, 'We played some superb football – just how I like to play and how I would like to see Swindon play,' a view that Gorman agreed with: 'The points were there for the taking. The standard of football was as good as you will see in the Second Division, and I felt we deserved a win.'

The match brought the first indication of a tactic which would prove to be trademark Hoddle. The move of Ross MacLaren to sweeper allowed both full-backs free licence to attack down the wings. Goals from Micky Hazard and Duncan Shearer twice clawed Town back from behind, before Shearer's second appeared to have won it. Then Viveash's gaffe put the cat among the pigeons.

A trip to Wolves the following Tuesday brought Hoddle's first win. Again coming back from a goal down, Shearer and Hazard once more supplied the goals in a 2-1 victory. Hazard's reaction was, 'It's amazing the difference a win makes. There is elation in the dressing room. The new management team deserve credit for keeping the spirits up.' Hoddle, meanwhile, said, 'Another couple of points and we will be well and truly safe and able to start building for next season.'

If only things were that simple.

A loss, a draw and a win in Hoddle's first three games had brought renewed optimism, but Swindon were still fifth from bottom. League re-organisation meant that just two teams would be relegated to the Third Division, and Swindon were just four points above second-bottom West Bromwich Albion with five games to play.

When the first of those five was lost at West Ham, then the next brought a defeat at home to Notts County, Swindon were just two points above the drop zone.

Immediately below them in the table were Leicester, who were due to visit the County Ground on 27 April. The Foxes had grabbed a draw at Sheffield Wednesday the previous midweek and were only below Town on goal difference. The match looked crucial for both clubs.

A Hazard penalty, an obliging own goal from the visitors and a Steve Foley hat-trick brought various things. It brought a 5-2 victory. It brought the only occasion of the season that Swindon had managed five goals. It brought three points, and it brought a four-point gap between the Robins and the trap door of relegation. But with two games and six points to play for, it still didn't bring safety.

Of the two final matches, Barnsley were up first and were two goals to the good with a minute of the first half remaining before another Hazard spot kick reduced the arrears. But to no avail; a 2-1 County Ground defeat. Only three points separated Swindon from the Third Division next season.

On the final day it would take an unlikely combined set of results, but theoretically Swindon could still join already relegated Hull in suffering the drop. However, their generally superior goal difference supplied a precious safety net.

Ultimately the Robins lost 3-1 at Port Vale and Leicester beat Oxford to draw level on points with Town. But West Brom's single point from a draw at Bristol Rovers condemned the Midlands side to follow Hull to the Third Division.

Town were safe in 21st place, two points above the drop zone and breathing a huge sigh of relief.

Over the season a huge persecution complex had grown, as suspicions were raised that Swindon were to be constructively relegated on the field of play through the intervention of match officials, so exercising the previous summer's intended demotion to the Third Division.

Such conspiracy theories are not unknown within the ranks of supporters. This time there seemed real evidence that the same thoughts existed within the offices of the County Ground.

But survive Town had. There had been a changing of the guard at the top, and as well respected and even loved as Ossie Ardiles had been, there was a belief that the installation of Glenn Hoddle at the helm would continue the playing style which had often promised so much success on the field.

3

1991/92

SWINDON TOWN supporters could have been forgiven for experiencing a feeling of déjà vu during the summer of 1991. Two years previously the club had appointed an ex-Tottenham Hotspur star, an international midfielder no less, as their player-manager and were hoping that their new man could take the team to the promised land of the First Division.

After the departure of Ossie Ardiles to Newcastle United a new campaign was on the horizon, and this time it was Glenn Hoddle who was tasked to lead the Robins into the rarefied air of the top flight.

The similarities in the respective pedigrees of Hoddle and Ardiles ran deep.

Born in Hayes in October 1957, Hoddle had joined Spurs' junior ranks as a 12-year-old, making his debut in the first team as a substitute five years later in 1975. In total, over 12 seasons he would take to the pitch on almost 500 occasions for Spurs, scoring a highly creditable 110 goals.

Voted PFA Young Player of the Year in 1979, he played in the FA Cup-winning team of 1981 and repeated the task 12 months later, scoring an extra-time goal against Queens Park Rangers in a 1-1 draw then a sixth-minute penalty for the only goal in the replay five days later.

While with Spurs he represented England throughout the 80s, appearing in two World Cups and two European Championships and gaining his 53rd and final cap in Euro 88, by which time he was performing for Monaco.

Hoddle scored nine times for his country over a nine-season international career, and fresh from taking over at Monaco, Arsène Wenger made Hoddle his top target, stealing his man from under the nose of similarly smitten Gérard Houllier at Paris Saint-Germain.

A four-season spell at Monaco followed, during which Hoddle made almost 90 appearances, averaging a goal every three.

Ardiles had joined Tottenham in 1978 after winning the World Cup in Argentina. By then, Hoddle had been an almost permanent fixture in the team for two seasons and the arrival of Ardiles gave Tottenham perhaps the most envied midfield in English football.

Ossie was employed by Tottenham for ten years, including a period in which his Spurs career was briefly placed on hold as he chose a season-long loan spell at Paris Saint-Germain in 1982 to escape potential diplomatic awkwardness arising through the Falklands conflict with Argentina.

They may have been born on different continents, they may have represented different international teams, but there was much similarity about Glenn Hoddle and Ossie Ardiles that deserved and survived close scrutiny.

Making almost 180 league starts together for the White Hart Lane club, they certainly had a comprehensive knowledge of each other's game and for many Spurs fans the midfield of the era was only complete when both appeared together.

There seemed to be other similarities. Ardiles had found his hands tied in the summer of 1990 as deliberation regarding Town's divisional status rumbled on for weeks, hampering his recruitment objectives. He would have identified with the financial challenges that replacement Hoddle was expected to contend with.

The fiscal constraints at the County Ground had been instrumental in convincing the Argentinian that his future lay elsewhere, and nothing had changed for the better ahead of Hoddle agreeing to take over.

In his autobiography, *Playmaker*, Hoddle explained that after undergoing a cartilage operation he had been offered the opportunity to regain some fitness by training at Chelsea, and there was a hint at some scouting work for manager Bobby Campbell.

At this stage it was assumed by most that his playing days were over, but a Chelsea reserve team game against Watford in March 1991 gave him his first chance to try out the success of both the medical procedure and his fitness work.

Mentally preparing for his first 90 minutes on a pitch for two years, he received a phone call from Peter Day, chief executive at Swindon, a man he knew from when both were at Tottenham Hotspur. Day got straight to the point, telling Hoddle that Swindon wanted him as their new manager.

While the call was both unexpected and welcome, Hoddle was at pains to point out that he was in no position to consider a player-manager role, but Day wasn't concerned, expressing the view that the appointment on offer was strictly on the basis of a non-playing manager.

After the game went without untoward incident, conversations continued to a successful conclusion with Hoddle being appointed on 4 April 1991.

He would have been well briefed on the monetary challenges ahead, so the relatively frugal business that was done during the summer would have been well received in the boardroom, and it was destined to have vast significance for many months to come.

On 25 July, Scottish-born Australian international striker Dave Mitchell was signed from Chelsea for a modest £30,000, and a day later a more eye-catching £200,000 was spent on Exeter City central defender Shaun Taylor. Those captures had been preceded by the re-signing of midfielder Martin Ling, who returned to the County Ground from Southend United for a bargain basement price of £15,000, five years after he had departed from his first stint at Swindon.

Three signings for a little under a quarter of a million pounds and only time would tell whether it was money well spent. Ossie Ardiles, looking on from Tyneside, could have been forgiven for asking why a figure of even these proportions had not been made available to him when he needed it.

But the day before the big kick-off brought news that Swindon had supplemented their playing staff with one of the biggest names in English football. After successfully completing a full pre-season training programme, Hoddle had been registered as a player and the Robins had just landed the biggest bargain of them all, for the vast sum of nothing.

Back in 1989 Ardiles had been appointed player-manager and went on to contribute a grand total of 50 minutes of playing time. Two seasons later, after doubts over his long-term fitness, Hoddle was initially appointed strictly as manager but was to go on to take to the pitch on 75 occasions. That's some piece of business.

Around the County Ground there was an understandable desire to move on to put recent events behind the club. A new image was needed to disassociate the future from the past.

Some changes were overblown and exaggerated, such as an announcement initially interpreted that Town were to take to the pitch for the forthcoming season in green shorts, resulting in outrage from traditionalists that the club's red and white heritage was being cast aside. The storm in a teacup was abated when it was revealed the change was to be little more than a minor trim addition, although the move to predominantly red shorts from white still had opposition to overcome.

The changing of the club badge, from the traditional railway engine logo of many decades to a modern simplistic letter 'S' within a diamond, was met with dismissive sniffiness from some. But the bigger plan was to use the new depiction to sell merchandise under the banner of Diamond Leisure, a new enterprise completely under the control of Swindon Town which would see all kit-sale proceeds go directly to the club, rather than to some multinational sportswear manufacturer.

New advertising and sponsorship opportunities were being explored, with Burmah climbing on board as main sponsors, and there were changes within the boardroom as Sir Seton Wills, a long-term supporter and benefactor, took his place among the directors.

A plan that seemed to have stalled was one that would have seen the demolition of the old Shrivenham Road Stand to be replaced with something that looked little more than a double decker row of portacabins, reducing the capacity of that side of the ground to just 1,300.

As new ground developments went it seemed an underwhelming indication of limited funds and limited ambition, and no one lamented the early disappearance of this particular scheme, but there was no doubt that there was a groundswell of intention to move on from the past.

A successful pre-season tournament in the Netherlands produced some silverware to show off, then Hoddle's contacts book was consulted and the visit of Spanish side Real Sociedad for an early August friendly ended in a 2-0 win for the visitors. Then a new season kicked off when Leicester City arrived at the County Ground on 17 August for the opening Second Division fixture of 1991/92.

With the 'top clubs' in the English football structure insisting that a 'Super League' was a necessity and with the authorities capitulating, this would be the last season in which the succinctly named Second Division would be considered the second level of English football. Swindon were aiming for change. The clubs in the First Division were demanding it.

'This season you will see a Swindon team playing a passing game,' said Hoddle in his first programme notes of the campaign. 'I'm sure it is the right approach, for the strength of the team we have is its passing ability. It's somewhat ironic that we should commence the serious business against Leicester City, for when we met them here in April it was a real crunch match in the battle to stay in the Second Division. We won 5-2 and in retrospect we can look back on that game as the turning point. That game saved us.'

That turning point had ultimately seen the Robins finish 21st and brought Second Division safety. This time, all supporters were hoping for a similar scoreline on the day and eventually a more successful season.

The outcome: a goalless draw. Compared to the 5-2 win, this was certainly not the direction in which everyone was hoping to turn.

'We were disappointed we did not get the win,' was Hoddle's post-match comment to the *Evening Advertiser*, 'but I thought we played some super passing football. All we needed was to show a bit more venom in our shooting to convert the chances we created.'

A week later, Duncan Shearer and a Micky Hazard penalty converted two of Town's chances at newly promoted Cambridge United. Meanwhile the U's converted three of their own.

Hoddle's subsequent assessment in his programme notes was, 'The Cambridge style is a very difficult system to play against, and John Beck's team take the long-ball style to further extremes than most sides. I can see few sides upsetting them on their own ground this season. But football has to win in the long run. If not, we might as well all pack in.'

One point from the first six was certainly a disappointment, but could hardly be considered a disaster, and when a two-legged League Cup victory over West Bromwich Albion brought a 4-2 aggregate passage to the second round things didn't look too bad.

Importantly, new signing Mitchell had already scored, Hazard had scored twice, and the established Shearer had already hit the back of the net three times. Shearer was on his way to his most prolific season in front of goal for Town. For the fourth season in a row none of his team-mates would outscore him, and for the last nine games of the campaign he would not even be a Swindon player at all.

Steve White scored his first of the season with the opening goal in a 3-1 home win over Barnsley as August ran out of days. White had been at Swindon since his capture by Lou Macari back in the summer of 1986 and had already hit the net almost 90 times.

Three days into September brought a trip to Ipswich Town and White was at it again. This time his third-minute opener preceded a convincing 4-1 away victory, a win Hoddle described as, 'Fantastic. We proved we can match and beat the best in the division and do it in style.'

Four days later Burslem was the destination for a 2-2 draw against Port Vale. White grabbed Town's first again and Hoddle was just as effusive, 'Football-wise we were excellent, but we failed to put the chances away. We could have been three or four goals up at half-time. If we don't do it this season and achieve promotion, then it will be games like this one which we will reflect back on as the reason why.'

The visit of Sunderland, whose promotion to the First Division in place of Swindon two seasons earlier had been followed by immediate relegation, to the County Ground midway through September might appear to bring a stiffer challenge. As was becoming traditional, White was again on the mark with Town's opener after eight minutes, and this time Swindon ran out winners by an entertaining 5-3 scoreline. Almost 11,500 fans were in attendance.

After attracting early criticism from the boss that his side were not converting enough of their chances, Swindon had scored 18 times over the most recent six league and cup games. As always, Shearer was his usual reliable self in front of goal, but an early season ankle ligament injury to Mitchell had presented the opportunity for White to show his indignation at starting the season as third-choice striker. A goal in each of four successive games had catapulted the 31-year-old back as a first-team regular.

With goals spread throughout the team, scoring had become the least of Town's problems. What required attention was the need for clean sheets.

The Robins sat in sixth place in the Second Division, top of a group of three teams on 11 points and occupying the last play-off place. Cambridge and Leicester, the two teams to whom Town had dropped points, sat second and third respectively while of local interest Bristol City lay fifth, and Bristol Rovers and Oxford United occupied the lowest two places in the table.

Throughout the mainly impressive start to the season, Hoddle had settled imperiously into the midfield. Always destined to be the star attraction whenever Swindon took to the road, the presence of the ex-England star would be responsible for many a club's highest home gate of the season.

But despite the likelihood of being overshadowed by the boss, Hazard and Shearer had starred in each of the two cup ties with West Brom, Martin Ling had scored with his second touch against Barnsley and central defenders Colin Calderwood and Shaun Taylor had immediately established an excellent rapport at the back which could only be augmented when both made the scoresheet away at Ipswich. This was no one-man team, and that was just as well.

On 17 September Tom Jones, who had been standing in at right-back for the injured David Kerslake since August, scored his first goal in two years in a 1-0 home victory over Bristol Rovers, and goalkeeper Nicky Hammond made his third start as Fraser Digby continued to recover from a knee injury. Hoddle's team's depth of squad was being tested.

Town had hoisted themselves up to third behind leaders Middlesbrough and dark horses Cambridge and had also kept their first clean sheet in the league for a month.

Generating little interest in Wiltshire at this point were Blackburn Rovers – recent beneficiaries of steel magnate Jack Walker's millions – who sat 14th. Walker had taken full control of the Ewood Park outfit in January. But the season was young; more of them later.

With almost weary familiarity White scored on the Robins' next outing, at Molineux as Town faced Wolverhampton Wanderers, but this time the goal was no more than an 87th-minute consolation in a first defeat in almost a month. Hoddle spoke of his disappointment that his side had not returned to Wiltshire with more to show for their efforts. Hazard had missed a penalty and Shearer was denied by the post, resulting in Wolves manager Graham Taylor expressing pleasant surprise that his side had claimed all three points.

The defeat also saw the return of David Kerslake to the bench after an eight-match absence through injury. His reappearance would allow Jones to return to midfield, start to settle the defence and see both men appear in all remaining 36 matches of the season. With Calderwood and Taylor having successfully stitched up the places in the centre of the back four, all that was left was to solve the problematic left-back position.

Watford's visit to the County Ground for the last match of September brought goals for Shearer, Fitzroy Simpson and Taylor, a windy and rainy 3-1 win for the home side and another three points for Hoddle's men.

Hammond, still in possession of the number one shirt ahead of the fit-again Digby, was considered the star of the show, but his heroics came at a cost with the keeper suffering torn stomach muscles early in the match.

Hoddle was confident in the style his new players were showing, saying later in the match programme, 'I doubt whether there are any sides in the Second Division that have the passing quality we possess. It's a skill which runs throughout the team, and it has been working very well for us.'

Music to the ears of Town supporters, who six months earlier had been nervous that the departure of Ossie Ardiles might spell the end of the assured football that they had become accustomed to witnessing.

The last week of September and first week of October proved to be a busy and productive time. In the League Cup, two first-half goals from the in-form Steve White had resulted in a 2-2 draw with Millwall, which also saw the dismissal of 20-year-old left-back Nicky Summerbee for receiving two yellow cards while Town held a two-goal advantage.

Again, the match had been notable for the performance of Hammond who performed manfully, protecting his goal for his ten-man side. The job was completed in a replay eight days into October when White was again on the scoresheet, ably assisted with a brace from Shearer, to see Swindon through to round three.

Fierce rivals Oxford were warmly welcomed to Swindon in the Full Members' Cup, resulting in an always celebrated victory for Town over their close neighbours. White maintained his incredible scoring run with another pair, Ross MacLaren chipped in with a third, but it still took penalties to determine the winner, Swindon deciding the evening from 12 yards by four spot kicks to three.

A single-goal defeat at Stamford Bridge in the fourth week of October eliminated Town at the hands of Chelsea in the next round. That just 5,784 attended the spectacle speaks volumes for the tournament's reputation.

With the Robins sitting third in the Second Division, things were looking very encouraging in their pursuit of promotion to the top tier. The goals were flowing, and the defence was looking significantly tighter than it had been in September.

For the first time since his arrival in the summer of 1987, Nicky Hammond was staking a creditable claim to be the starting goalkeeper, with appearances split almost evenly between the ex-Arsenal man and Sheffield-born Fraser Digby.

A twice-broken leg had earlier robbed the Londoner of two whole seasons in recovery. However, with Hammond suffering injury, a recall for Digby would prove just how useful it was to have two capable and in-form goalkeepers, and a trip to relegation-threatened Plymouth Argyle would be a good test of the new-found security of the Robins' defence.

A clean sheet at Home Park would seem to answer that conundrum, and the feelgood factors at the other end of the pitch also continued as Duncan Shearer decided that he'd had enough of partner Steve White stealing the limelight.

Braces of goals either side of half-time for the Scotsman were a bigger talking point than the torn thigh muscle which saw Hoddle leave the pitch in the 65th minute. It was the first time the man known as Postman Pat had struck four times in a match since joining Swindon back in the summer of 1988, and it took Shearer's seasonal tally over all competitions to double figures, overtaking White.

One of Shearer's goals was slotted in from a tight angle after pouncing on a sloppy backpass. Another left Argyle keeper Rhys Wilmot helpless on the floor as he rounded the custodian to net the concluding strike. The result meant that Swindon were the highest-scoring team in any of the top four divisions.

Hoddle said on local TV, 'It was the Duncan Shearer show. He had six chances and scored four. We've played a lot better this season, but the ironic thing is we've played better, created more chances and lost games.'

Shearer, signed for £250,000 by Lou Macari, had scored more than 60 goals over the previous three seasons, and he was showing no sign of reducing his output. Such consistent deadliness in front of goal would be crucial to Town's aims for 1991/92 and would not go unnoticed by rivals.

Ahead of a home fixture with Derby County in mid-October, Hoddle's programme notes again praised his team's top scorer, 'Duncan monopolised the headlines with his four goals at Plymouth, but I thought his all-round play against Millwall was even better. It was his best performance for the club since I arrived and his partnership with Steve White seems to be getting stronger every week.'

Shearer was proving to be the huge goalscoring asset that supporters had known he would be for some time, and four in one game was bound to attract attention from covetous rival managers. If Hoddle was only just becoming aware of his predatory ability, was it wise to broadcast the fact more widely than necessary?

If there was any value in anonymity, neither Shearer nor White found the net in the 2-1 home defeat to Derby on 12 October, a first County Ground loss of the season. Micky Hazard struck an equalising penalty, but with the injured Hoddle not pulling the strings the Robins failed to find their usual fluidity.

Digby could do nothing to prevent the ball deflecting off Shaun Taylor and into his net for Derby's opener but

Hazard beat visiting goalkeeper Peter Shilton to level. Then it was Digby who was at fault, racing out to cut out a long ball, failing to gather it effectively and being powerless to stop the promotion-chasing Rams netting the winner.

The defeat was Town's third of the season.

Good news came the following week that Swindon's financial position had apparently taken a huge turn for the better as the annual accounts were published. A deficit of over £500,000 the previous year had been turned into a £500,000 profit, with the improvement almost entirely due to the £1m sale of Alan McLoughlin to Southampton. All told, almost £1.7m had arrived in Town's coffers as a result of transfer dealings.

While plainly very welcome additional income, and surely the sort of monetary upturn that Ossie Ardiles could only have dreamed of, it was an inescapable fact that each departing player was inevitably likely to result in a weakened team.

When McLoughlin had left Wiltshire for the south coast in December 1990 Swindon were five points off a play-off spot. Six months later the Robins escaped relegation by just two points. Balancing financial prudence against footballing success requires a never-ending sleight of hand.

It was in this light that Swindon welcomed Blackburn to the County Ground on 19 October. The hosts were fourth in the table on 20 points with almost a quarter of the league season played. Meanwhile, over the previous month Rovers had climbed four places to eighth but were still two points worse off than the Robins.

Jack Walker had splashed some of his cash to appoint Liverpool legend Kenny Dalglish and his assistant Ray

Harford as a managerial double act, and the trip to Wiltshire would be the first test of the new dream team.

After a goalless first half, the deadlock was broken 20 minutes into the second period. A Tom Jones corner was flicked on at the near post, Colin Calderwood's attempted shot didn't trouble visiting keeper Bobby Mimms, but the predatory Steve White swooped to score his first league goal in four outings.

The restored Nicky Hammond couldn't hold a shot and David Speedie fired home an equaliser from the loose ball, but skipper Calderwood stabbed home the winner two minutes into added time after Mimms didn't grasp a shot from White.

Towards the end of October, a brace of Shearer goals for no reply at Brighton, coupled with a Hammond penalty save, continued the good run. Then a convincing 4-1 away win at Third Division Huddersfield Town in the League Cup secured safe passage to round four, ex-Huddersfield man Shearer scoring twice. Nicky Summerbee scored the first goal of his career, and it also brought a traditional Shaun Taylor headed goal.

Then November commenced in similar winning fashion when Ossie Ardiles's Newcastle arrived in Swindon and capitulated to the tune of a 2-1 defeat.

Again, the goals came from Calderwood and White, giving Town their third win on the trot and lifting them to second in the table. The result left the Magpies just one point off the Second Division relegation zone, and by the time the two teams met again in March, Ardiles was gone.

Things were certainly looking encouraging for Hoddle and his team, and the boss had said as much in his programme notes, 'The quality of our approach play is being admired by people at all levels in the game including the supporters of our opponents. Things are looking so good for us at the moment, but we must not fall into the trap of complacency. If we keep churning out quality performances, then nine times out of ten the results will follow. Our style is very continental, and our opponents seem to have trouble dealing with it.'

Continuing, Hoddle said, 'Everyone has worked extremely hard, and no one has shied away from grafting both on the training field and on a Saturday afternoon. But they must not get carried away by the plaudits. Only a certain amount of the job has been done. There is so much more for us to achieve.'

Perhaps prophetically, he finished, 'It's not going to be easy – success doesn't come cheap.'

So, summarising Hoddle's assessment, people were watching Swindon Town, they were admiring their players and money would be a factor. Hmm.

No one at the time knew that the league victory over Newcastle would be the last three-point haul for two months.

And even then, while a 0-0 shut-out at Charlton was the first time Swindon hadn't scored in 14 matches, the point took them to the very summit of the Second Division, overhauling Cambridge and Middlesbrough by the superior goal difference that all those goals from Shearer and White had brought.

At first the goals kept coming, and from the expected sources. A goal each from White and Shearer at Southend weren't enough to overcome the three scored by the home side as November continued. Then two more from White at home against Portsmouth couldn't stop Swindon sliding to the second home defeat of the season by the same scoreline.

And perhaps alarmingly, after 15 goals in total, White had already scored his last of the season for Town with almost six months still to run. Not only that, even though Dave Mitchell was finally looking towards recovering fitness having missed the last three months, it would be the second month of 1992 before his name would be seen on the scoresheet.

Another 0-0 stalemate at Tranmere Rovers was followed by a further five successive draws as the points continued to slip through the Robins' fingers between the end of November to New Year's Day.

Bradford-on-Avon-born and Melksham-bred Fitzroy Simpson was revelling in the attacking midfield role that Hoddle was encouraging, and he scored in the 1-1 home draw with Grimsby Town, then again in the 2-2 draw at Middlesbrough, which saw Shearer record his first in four matches. Another goalless outcome at home to Ipswich Town was followed by a Shearer goal in the 1-1 Boxing Day encounter at Bristol City, and Shearer again made the scoresheet in the 1-1 deadlock at Barnsley three days before New Year's Eve.

The optimist could argue that Swindon had remained undefeated for six matches, but the realist would observe that over their last eight outings they had tumbled from the pinnacle of the table to ninth.

Looking back, from and including the last match in September to the first in November, Town had played six times, scored 14 goals and taken 15 points. There had been six different names on the scoresheet. Only five goals had been conceded and there had been two clean sheets.

Now, throughout six matches in November and December, just five goals had been scored, spread across just two scorers. Six points had been collected, but just as earlier, five goals had been conceded and there were two clean sheets.

The defence looked as secure as ever. It looked like Hoddle's earlier observation that his team were not capitalising on their chances sufficiently was coming true once more.

While Swindon were still only four points off a play-off place, there were four clubs level on 41 points at the top of the division, separated only by goal difference. Surprise package Cambridge still topped the cluster, accompanied by Ipswich and Middlesbrough. The fourth member of the elite group of four were Blackburn, who had steadily climbed the table to make a serious promotion challenge.

The season was exactly halfway through and 1992 was about to dawn. What would the new year bring?

With Hoddle still injured, the boss had been unable to influence things on the pitch since the beginning of October. That had been a huge loss, but the unfortunate situation had opened up an opportunity for the seasoned Ross MacLaren to step into. Now in his fourth season in Wiltshire, MacLaren had been asked to demonstrate his perception and range of passing skills to mitigate against the loss of the player-manager, and he was coping admirably. Many were seeing the established defender of over 125 Town appearances in a new light.

The central defensive partnership of Shaun Taylor and Colin Calderwood had flowered into a formidable duo. Taylor had suffered an injury in November, but the four matches missed would be the only absences for the former Exeter City man. No such problems for the consistent

Calderwood, who would appear an astonishing 57 times by the end of the campaign in May.

Also in defence, David Kerslake was proving just the sort of right-back who suited Hoddle's wing-back ideals, missing half a dozen games through September but otherwise on course to remain in place until 4 May. The left-back position was still proving more troublesome, with Adi Viveash occupying the slot for a few early games before deputising for the injured Taylor.

Come 1992 Nicky Summerbee had mostly worn the number three shirt but with the new year approaching midfielder Tom Jones, having previously filled in at right-back to cover for Kerslake, was being forced into the more defensive role.

Up front, the injury to newcomer Mitchell would go virtually unnoticed all the time Shearer and White continued to hit the back of the net. But with the 15-goal White destined to be goal-barren to the end of the season, pressure would be on the returning Mitchell to step up to the plate.

The other striking option was that of Shaun Close, at that stage, two and a half years a Swindon player. His one goal so far had arrived in the League Cup around 14 months earlier. His second, and last, was still to come.

No such problems with the goal return of Shearer. With 22 in all competitions to the turn of the year, Shearer had yet to miss a game. His contribution was proving vital in Town's campaign, and that would become even more plain by the season's end.

In midfield was Micky Hazard, whose performances had brought many man-of-the-match nominations and who had played every match so far. The versatile Tom Jones was usually an engine room partner when not filling in at either of the full-back positions, and local boy Fitzroy Simpson was showing the sort of development that the tutelage of an ex-England midfielder might hope to bring.

And between the posts, Nicky Hammond was at last able to challenge long-term regular Fraser Digby for possession of the (notionally) green shirt. Injury had mostly been responsible for restricting Hammond's league appearances to just nine over four years. By the season's end he had added a further 25 to that total and outstripped the 21 that Digby would make.

Those options for Hoddle may have been akin to those faced by England managers when forced to choose between Peter Shilton and Ray Clemence, such were the rare occasions when two such capable goalkeepers were vying for the same shirt (some might consider that analogy a little over-imaginative).

So, as 1992 dawned and with defensive security being questioned, it's important to mention the previous season's much-heralded signing.

Néstor Lorenzo had arrived at the behest of fellow Argentinian Ossie Ardiles and had impressed with composed, if sometimes a little over-zealous, performances.

Hoddle had picked the defender in four of his first eight games in charge at the tail end of 1990/91 but come the start of 1992 he had failed to select Lorenzo in the starting line-up of any game since. On the face of it, the World Cup runner-up seemed ideally suited to the style of game that Hoddle wanted Swindon to play. The manager appeared to think otherwise.

Destined to stay on the sidelines until March, Lorenzo then took to the pitch three times and each one was lost, including a heavy and humiliating defeat at Oxford. He was an unused substitute in a win over Tranmere in the middle of the month and he then left the club in the summer.

Understandably the major draw for Lorenzo to sign for Swindon had been to join up with Ardiles, but to play for Hoddle must surely have had some sort of appeal itself.

It appeared that Hoddle wanted to use the Buenos Aires-born man in a more forward role, perhaps more so than the man himself felt comfortable. But John Gorman would comment later that it was Lorenzo himself who wanted to over-commit himself in an attacking manner, leaving his defence exposed.

Either Hoddle didn't rate him, he wasn't as good as we thought, he just plainly wanted away, or he blotted his copybook through his attitude. Lorenzo's disciplinary record was certainly questionable. In July he signed for Argentinian side San Lorenzo de Almagro – surely the most appropriately named destination for a football man until Arsène Wenger joined Arsenal in 1996.

So, to New Year's Day 1992 and the visit of Millwall to the County Ground. Dave Mitchell made his first start up front since the second game of the season, with the perhaps unfortunate Steve White dropped to the bench.

Duncan Shearer took the pressure off anyone suffering post festive season trepidation with his third and fourth goals in a week. In between Martin Ling contributed his first strike since August, with all the goals coming in the first half. The year was up and running with a 3-1 win.

Three days later, Second Division rivals Watford visited the County Ground in the third round of the FA Cup. The game matched old Spurs team-mates Hoddle and

Steve Perryman as opposing managers. England under-21 goalkeeper David James was the Hornets' stopper, former England striker Luther Blissett supplied the danger up front and future Swindon defender Jason Drysdale was at left-back.

For the home side, White was again on the bench, Mitchell again took his place on the field, and Shearer again scored twice. This time his strikes bookended the encounter, the first coming just four minutes in and the second ten minutes from the end, with Mitchell grabbing his first since the League Cup match against West Brom back in August after ten minutes.

Mitchell's goal was the pick of the crop, bulleting home a header from a Shearer cross after an exquisitely swift passing move, while Shearer's second was completed despite having suffered a broken nose in a first-half collision.

Blissett scored twice for the visitors to level, but to no avail. Thanks to Shearer's late winner Town were through to the fourth round where they would meet Cambridge on 25 January.

Before that, Cambridge needed to make the trip to the County Ground in a Second Division fixture, the reverse encounter of the second game of the season. That one had seen Town lose 3-2. This time two Cambridge goals without reply sufficed for the three points to wend their way back to the Abbey Stadium.

Steve White was named on the bench, from where he replaced Fitzroy Simpson, but it would be the last time he would be seen on the pitch until the following August. A persistent back injury would need attention, and the scorer of 15 goals had been lost from the front line for the rest of the season.

Tom Jones had again taken the left-back position, weakening his potential midfield contribution, but that was about to change: on 9 January it was announced that the problem with the bothersome position was about to be resolved.

Back in March 1991, Paul Bodin's departure to Crystal Palace had produced repercussions that were still being felt. Firstly, Adi Viveash was offered the number three shirt, which didn't immediately seem to play to the strengths of someone more accustomed to a centre-back role.

As 1991/92 developed and with Hoddle stamping his midfield influence on Town's style of play, the wing-back needs of the left-back position were very different to those usually associated with a flat back four defence.

Nicky Summerbee was offered the opportunity, and the youngster grabbed it admirably, initially making the position his own as he demonstrated the attacking wing play so reminiscent of his father Mike in Swindon days gone by. But to some it seemed an anathema that the Summerbee name wasn't being used solely in an attacking role, free of defensive duties.

So the announcement that Bodin was about to return to the County Ground solved an issue which had first been suffered by Ardiles, and then for ten months by Hoddle.

Bodin said to the *Swindon Evening Advertiser*, 'It's the end of a nightmare. I feel as though I have wasted ten months of my career. I can't wait to get started again at Swindon.'

The transfer of the Welsh international to Crystal Palace had been completed in return for a fee of £550,000 and had contributed to the disenchantment of Ardiles. The stagnation of Bodin's career at Selhurst Park had brought about a reduction in his value, which when deducted from the outstanding fee remaining to be paid by the London club meant that just £50,000 was believed to have changed hands to bring Bodin back west.

Denying there had ever been a falling out with Palace boss Steve Coppell, Bodin blamed a contrast in styles between Palace's game and his own preferences. Having spent the last few weeks on loan to Newcastle, still under the management of Ardiles, he reminisced that he had been reluctant to leave Swindon and that the sale had been dictated by the club's poor financial state: 'It was a bad time to go. I thought we had a chance of repeating the success of the previous season, but then the side began to break up. I loved the football under Ossie Ardiles, and I know Glenn Hoddle holds similar beliefs. That made Swindon top of my list.'

Paul's recollections later in the book provide a more detailed insight.

Meanwhile, elsewhere in the national press, comparisons were being made between England striker Alan Shearer at Southampton and namesake Duncan. The more celebrated man had scored 15 times for the Saints. Duncan had already notched 24 for Town. It was just the sort of attention and speculation that the club, supporters and manager could do without.

It took just 74 minutes for the returning Bodin to celebrate his homecoming with his first goal. A free kick on the edge of the Leicester box was knocked sideways to be arrowed home by Bodin, but by then the game was long lost, the home side already holding a three-goal lead.

A week later, the FA Cup fourth round tie with Cambridge had been built up as a clash of styles between the opposing managers Hoddle and John Beck, one renowned for a cultured passing game while the other often ridiculed for his long-ball methods.

Such comparisons and judgements are often disrespectful towards the circumstances under which each club operates, but Hoddle allowed for little doubt in which direction his own footballing beliefs pointed him. Speaking after the convincing 3-0 win at the Abbey Stadium, he said, 'We were aware of the great contrasts in style, and I'm pleased to say that football has won the day. It's taken three games for me to be able to say that, and I'm very pleased it's finally happened.'

Micky Hazard, who had been critical of Cambridge's tactics before, said, 'This has to be the most satisfying win of the season.'

Colin Calderwood had opened the scoring with Shearer adding his by now customary brace, giving Town a passage to round five, and doing something to avenge the six points lost to the U's in the league. It was as far as they had progressed in the FA Cup since 1970.

As satisfied as Hazard had been with the victory of methods achieved over Cambridge, many supporters would have looked to the last fixture in January as one which would define contentment more completely. That's because Oxford visited the County Ground and left with no points after goals from Kerslake and Shearer helped record a 2-1 victory.

The result left Oxford six points adrift at the bottom of the Second Division table, with Town eighth and two points off a play-off place.

It was Kerslake's first goal for the club on his 109th appearance, on a cold night when visibility was so poor that referee Keren Barratt took a long, hard look before deciding the match could proceed. Thankfully for Swindon he did because at the end Hoddle enthused, 'The quality of passing right through the team here is as good as I've known at places like Monaco and Spurs. I firmly believe that only Manchester United and Leeds are better footballing sides than us.' Praise indeed.

He added, 'We know we are always capable of scoring goals, so if we can stop the flow at the other end we should still be in with a shout in May.' Shearer's season's total stood at 27. What if they stopped?

And next up was a trip to Ewood Park to face Blackburn, who were converting Jack Walker's millions into points so successfully that they sat at the very top of the table.

For the third time in four matches, Swindon surrendered a goal lead, achieved from a Dave Mitchell strike four minutes before half-time. The score was still 1-0 with 15 minutes remaining when, after Swindon had dominated their multi-million-pound opponents for so long, Dalglish made the sort of substitutions that managers with money at their disposal can make.

On came striker Simon Garner, and central defender Colin Hendry was thrown on up front alongside him as Dalglish threw caution to the wind. Hendry's shot took a lucky deflection off Calderwood to beat Digby for the equaliser, then David Speedie grabbed the winner with seven minutes to go.

The defeat was rough justice for Town, who had forced Blackburn goalkeeper Bobby Mimms into some desperate action, but they had failed to capitalise on their superior opportunities.

Rovers midfielder Gordon Cowans told the press afterwards, 'Swindon are the best Second Division side I have seen. They are well organised and more than matched us in every department. They must feel sick at this result.'

Hoddle, meanwhile, philosophised, 'That was a real heartbreaker. It was probably the most disappointing result of our season so far. We had the chances to wrap the game up by half-time but did not make the most of them. I still think we were the better side.'

The defeat left Town ninth, while leaders and upwardly mobile Blackburn were nine points ahead and seemingly destined for automatic promotion.

Consecutive home fixtures against Bristol City and Brighton brought some respite, although the upturn would prove to be temporary.

A pride-restoring 2-0 win over the Robins of Bristol achieved from Tom Jones's first goal in two years and the ubiquitous Shearer's 28th of the season was followed by three points gained from a 2-1 win over the Seagulls.

Trailing with 20 minutes to go, Calderwood's two strikes were not the usual fodder of central defenders. First he played a one-two with Hazard, collecting the return on his chest and placing a shot past Perry Digweed in off a post, then he timed a run to perfection to crash a volley off the underside of the bar to seal the win.

Approaching the midway point of February, Town were not giving up on the promotion hunt. Back up to fourth, a final position of a play-off place was within grasp once more with 16 matches remaining.

League pressures were relieved with the FA Cup fifth round tie against First Division Aston Villa in front of the TV cameras. It was estimated that ten million viewers watched Ron Atkinson's side run out 2-1 winners at the County Ground, with the finishing of Dwight Yorke and

Steve Froggatt proving decisive, overcoming Mitchell's 76th-minute attempt to redress a losing position.

But when it came back down to the nitty-gritty of Second Division promotion aspirations with a trip to Grimsby in the last week of February, perhaps things started to get the better of Hoddle's men. The long haul to Blundell Park brought just one point in a goalless affair, and then four defeats on the trot followed.

There was little shame in defeat at Newcastle, perhaps more disappointment with home losses to Middlesbrough and Charlton Athletic, but the loss of face in a humiliating reverse at Oxford was probably the most painful to bear for Swindon supporters.

For them, the game was notable for three reasons. Firstly, the appearance of Néstor Lorenzo from the bench would be the first time he had been seen on a pitch since August. Secondly, for Hoddle's much awaited return, which was greeted with far more enthusiasm by the travelling Town fans. And thirdly, the almost disbelief that Shaun Close would start a match and score a goal. That Close's strike should be recorded at just 32 seconds after kick-off somehow compounded the incredulity that he might be attempting to make up for lost time.

Two goals from Dave Mitchell were ultimately cancelled out by a pair from the Oxford-born, Oxford United-supporting Joey Beauchamp, leaving his team, who had started the afternoon second from bottom, with a 5-3 victory.

The win lifted the U's out of the relegation places, and the fleeting afternoon of *Twilight Zone*-esque action culminated two months later when the three points gained were ultimately the difference between Second Division safety and relegation to the third tier for the Manor Ground club.

But back in the real world, reality had struck as March commenced, the month during which all transfer activity had to conclude for players to be eligible to play for their new clubs during the ongoing season. Traditionally, transfer deadline day was one of excitement and trepidation for fans, with the latter often being the case when related to Swindon.

On 3 March it was announced that rising star Fitzroy Simpson was to join Manchester City in return for £550,000 and was off to play in the Premier League, which would commence its inaugural season in less than six months.

The news was received with a mixture of weary expectation and resigned acceptance. The fee was significant enough that it plainly couldn't be ignored by the board. Simpson had made big strides under Hoddle, but his departure was nothing more than had been encountered and ultimately overcome in the past, such as with the loss of Alan McLoughlin 18 months earlier.

But it was the departure of McLoughlin which had fuelled the disillusionment of manager Ossie Ardiles. The loss of the talented Simpson, ever-present that season bar two matches missed through suspension and who had contributed four goals, would do nothing to enhance promotion ambitions.

How would this deal affect not only the performance of the team, but the commitment of Hoddle? Would any of the incoming fee be made available to the boss to use to bolster the freshly depleted numbers?

Then rumours that new Newcastle manager Kevin Keegan coveted right-back David Kerslake brought predictable angry letters in the local press. An offer was rejected and Kerslake publicly stated that he was eager to remain in Wiltshire, 'The gaffer has made me aware of Newcastle's interest but I'm certainly not looking to get away. I am quite happy to stay.'

Under a *Swindon Evening Advertiser* banner of 'I Will Buy Kerslake', it was reported that Keegan's offer had fallen short of Swindon's £500,000 valuation, with the former England forward commenting, 'I was led to believe that I could get him at a price, less than Swindon want. The gap is not too great, and I still hope to sign him before the weekend.'

The *Advertiser* finished with the comment, 'Despite a transfer market profit approaching £2m since November 1989, Swindon are still looking to cut costs. The right offer would be difficult to resist.'

Any hope that some of the incoming cash from Simpson's sale could be used for team-building seemed to be just so much wishful thinking. The ruckus preceded Swindon's trip to St James' Park, where Kerslake appeared for Town and a Mitchell goal couldn't prevent a 3-1 defeat.

So, under all such disquieting business action, what was needed was a return to business-as-usual on the pitch. Mid-table Tranmere came to the County Ground on a Tuesday night, Shearer scored twice, Digby kept a clean sheet, and all was right in the world.

Hoddle, in his fourth match since returning from injury, opted for a five-man defence, which kept Rovers striker John Aldridge quiet, and Mitchell ran the visitors' defence ragged with his industrious endeavours.

The following Saturday, Southend United arrived in Wiltshire. Fourteen minutes in, Shearer started the afternoon with his third goal in four days, Bodin then added a penalty and Mitchell gained reward for his previous efforts with his own strike. The Shrimpers had netted an equaliser to make the score 1-1, but that was ultimately inconsequential. The Robins overtook Southend in the table and with nine matches remaining they were again two points short of the last play-off place.

It was 21 March and there were six weeks of the season left. Time for another disquieting financial update.

Details regarding Swindon's financial status were released to the press, explaining that a £600,000 wage bill increase, agreed before Wembley play-off success in 1990, had still needed to be honoured regardless of demotion. There was no money available and there were just days until the transfer deadline.

To Swindon supporters this all felt like damage limitation, information leakage. And so it was.

Under the headline 'Kenny grabs goal king Duncan', the *Western Daily Press* reported on 24 March that Blackburn boss Dalglish had splashed £750,000 to take Swindon's talismanic marksman to Lancashire. At the time, Rovers were two points clear at the top of the table.

Shearer, who had drawn level with Town legend Don Rogers' goalscoring record with his 32nd of the season against Southend, was no longer a goalscoring asset. The loan signings of Gary Waddock from QPR and Terry Gibson from Wimbledon seemed scant compensation, although the astute capture of John Moncur from Tottenham for £80,000 increased and enhanced the Spurs connection at the County Ground.

What now for the season? The answer was supremely predictable.

Over the remaining nine games, while just one was lost, Swindon failed to score more than once in any of them.

Goalless draws at Watford and Sunderland brought a couple of points, and 1-1 scorelines achieved at Portsmouth, Millwall and Bristol Rovers, all creditable in their own right, were not likely to bring the points necessary to do more than stabilise the Robins just outside the play-off zone.

Home wins over Port Vale, Wolves and Plymouth were welcome but sadly lacking in impact. Town remained cemented in eighth, two off the last play-off spot. The final game, away at Derby, brought a 2-1 defeat, confirmed the Rams' third-placed finish and brought the curtain down on the campaign.

In truth, the final whistle of Swindon's season may well have been blown the moment Duncan Shearer put pen to paper on a contract with Blackburn back in March.

The most notable performances in the run-in were taking place at Ewood Park. From the moment Shearer became a Rovers player, Kenny Dalglish's Blackburn went into free-fall.

With six consecutive losses, inclusive of a home defeat against Charlton the week before Shearer's arrival at Ewood, they plummeted from top of the table to seventh. Then a couple of wins and two draws sealed sixth place and entered a breathless and nervous team into the play-offs.

Back in Swindon it didn't take too long to realise just what Dalglish had done with Jack Walker's money.

Shearer had been signed not to add firepower to Blackburn's front line but to deprive Swindon's of it. He appeared in six games, scored one goal and left the club for Aberdeen in the summer, recouping much of the outlay. His place was taken at Ewood Park with the purchase of Alan Shearer before the first ball of the following season was kicked.

Duncan's recollections make for fascinating reading later in this book.

Victory over Derby in the play-off semi-finals, coupled with a win at Wembley over Leicester, took Blackburn Rovers to the new Premier League and paved the way for a Walker-inspired title in 1995.

Jealousy is not an attractive quality. After all, who wouldn't want their team to be able to outbid their rivals to the best talent available?

Perhaps Swindon supporters had just experienced the effect of the financial clout that everyone was to become used to with the imminent formation of the Premier League, but this was a blatant victory for chequebook strategy.

Hoddle admitted, 'Selling Duncan Shearer could have cost us promotion,' a view that most observers already subscribed to, and an action which so many fans had feared for much of the season.

During the summer it seemed that another issue had finally been put to bed, as Winchester Crown Court was the venue for a fixture which, this time, did not appear to involve Swindon Town Football Club at all.

The Inland Revenue's case against various individuals brought much debate, which over the course of six weeks saw the conclusion of the financial irregularity scandal that had rocked the club for years.

There was more airing of dirty linen than is necessary to retell within the pages of a football book, with the upshot that Lou Macari was cleared of tax fraud charges.

Perhaps, finally, the time was right for a line to be drawn under the proceedings which had brought so many sleepless nights for so many people who held the Robins in their affections.

Certainly, chairman Ray Hardman felt so. 'From today we start again,' he told the *Advertiser.* 'Let's have a good season with everyone pulling in the same direction. We have two weeks to go to the start of the new season. What we have to do is back Glenn Hoddle and John Gorman to do whatever is sensibly necessary to create a side that will get us into the Premier League.'

Time to move on. Let success and failure be determined on the football pitch once again.

Swindon's 1991/92 season could in no way be considered a failure. Twentieth in the table after two matches, the first week in November had seen them briefly top the division. But from then on it was the Robins' lot to stay between fourth and tenth, sometimes flirting with a play-off place, sometimes aspiring to reach them.

A rookie manager had been blooded, a league finish of eighth was a 13-place improvement on the previous season and the panache that Hoddle's side had demonstrated had often been marvellous to watch.

Surely the boardroom could only be satisfied with what seemed inevitable and vital book balancing, but every supporter was left with a taste of 'what might have been'. Just as they had experienced after demotion two seasons previously.

Two years had passed since Ossie Ardiles's team had been denied promotion to the First Division, and while supporters had been forced to live with that pain, there was still a burning ache to right the perceived wrongs and claim the place at the top table, which was just about to be renamed the Premier League

What for Hoddle's second full campaign?

4
1992/93

AUGUST 1992 was halfway through before football resumed at the County Ground. Glenn Hoddle was facing his second full season as player-manager and hopes were high.

There had been many encouraging signs the previous campaign and time would tell whether the play-off place that had proved just out of reach in 1991/92 could be attained, or whether finishing eighth would prove to be a high-water tide mark.

Hoddle had fielded questions regarding his position at Swindon even as the previous season had ended, 'There is no hiding the disappointment at missing out on Premier League football. After selling Duncan Shearer we were unbeaten apart from the last game. You could say the revenue from the play-offs might have been more than the £750,000 we got from the sale of Duncan.

'We can't go into the new season with only two strikers. I hope [the still injured] Steve White will fully recover, but at the moment we desperately need a striker who is going to come in and do a good job for us.'

And on speculation that Spurs may come calling for his services, he said, 'I just want to keep on with the job here and take things as they come. There is a lot of hype about this, and I honestly think it's the Spurs crowd more than anything. I spent 13 happy years at Spurs and in some ways, I was idolised by some sections of the crowd.

'They have seen the things I have done here at Swindon, put two and two together and said, "That is the sort of style Tottenham have been brought up on." If anything comes out of it, we'll wait and see and take that decision when it comes.'

Transfer activity during the close-season had been minimal, but one signing which did take place would prove to be decisive, particularly as at the top of Hoddle's wish list was a striker.

Midfielder Tom Jones, at the County Ground since 1988, had turned down a new contract offer in March, an action which had led to the signing of John Moncur the same month. Informed by Hoddle that he would not now be considered a first-choice option, Jones, who had been almost ever-present the previous season, told the *Evening Advertiser*, 'I always said that if things could have been sorted out, I would rather have remained at Swindon, but I'm clearly better off elsewhere.'

The situation was resolved when Jones moved to Reading, with striker Craig Maskell heading the opposite way along the M4.

The transfer might have been slightly acrimonious on Jones's part, but Maskell was to hit the ground running. There had been a huge hole created by the departure of Duncan Shearer the previous March and Maskell had big boots to fill.

But the newcomer knew what he was up against. Maskell had followed Shearer before, moving to Huddersfield Town to replace him when the Scotsman moved to the Robins in 1988. In his excellent book *The Register*, Swindon Town statistician Paul Plowman detailed that as an 18-year-old, Maskell, at the time signed to Southampton, once spent a loan spell at Swindon under Lou Macari and scored four goals in a reserve win at Portsmouth but was denied a first-team start.

Maskell scored six times in 12 days over April 1987 at Swindon but it took another five years and a deal featuring Tom Jones and £250,000 for him to become a full-time Town player.

The other incoming player would make a significant contribution over a five-season stay, bringing in a seven-figure fee when he moved on: Kevin Horlock joined on a free transfer from West Ham United in August.

Ironically, the formation of the Premier League meant that Town had reached the status for which the club had striven since 1879, as the Football League structure underwent a renaming process. The Second Division was reclassified as the First Division, and Swindon kicked off season 1992/93 as a First Division club.

And on 15 August, visiting the County Ground for the season's opener, were Sunderland, beaten in the previous season's FA Cup Final by Liverpool; the team the Robins had defeated in the play-off final at Wembley in 1990 before all sorts of retribution rained on their parade.

Maskell started up front alongside Dave Mitchell, recent arrival John Moncur formed a third of a midfield trio with Micky Hazard and Martin Ling, and sweeper Glenn Hoddle achieved what he hadn't managed so far during his reign and scored.

In the 55th minute, Hoddle dummied a Sunderland defender and struck the sweetest of 30-yard strikes to leave Tony Norman helpless. The keeper was having a busy afternoon fending off attempts from various Town sources, none better than a rasping right-footed volley from left-back Paul Bodin.

He had already foiled an earlier Hoddle curler, and while the conquest of Norman might not have been a Groundhog Day of Wembley 26 months earlier, the final score had a familiar ring: Swindon Town 1 Sunderland 0.

Hoddle's pre-match programme notes referred to maintaining the style and system that had brought an eighth-placed finish and teasingly promised 'one or two tactical variations we have introduced' which were apparently 'so subtle I doubt whether you will pick them up, and hopefully the opposition won't either'.

That may have run the risk of talking down to the supporters. Come the end of the season, however, fans had forgotten about any potential of feeling patronised.

Four days later came a local derby at Twerton Park, still the stadium that Bristol Rovers shared with Bath City. The game saw the first airing of a summer rule change, which outlawed goalkeepers handling a ball passed back to them by a team-mate.

The clock showed 88 minutes when Fraser Digby appeared to smuggle a ball over the goal line without using his hands. Referee Keith Burge consulted his linesman, the pair disagreeing with Digby's interpretation and awarding Rovers an indirect free kick on the six-yard line.

With the entire Swindon team lined up on the goal line, the initial shot was blocked but the rebound was crashed home through the wall. That made the score an incredible 4-3 to Town with only added time remaining.

All four of their goals had come in the first 47 minutes. Shaun Taylor had netted after just three, Mitchell getting the next before ex-Bath man Bodin added a penalty, with Rovers clawing back a reply just before half-time. Mitchell claimed his second as the second half began, but Marcus Stewart reduced the arrears on the hour. Paul Hardyman's late, late strike brought about a frantic finish which saw the Robins survive.

Two matches, five goals and six points. A good start, which was compounded at Molineux with a 2-2 draw against Wolverhampton Wanderers the following Saturday. Shaun Taylor's 83rd-minute header appeared to have claimed all three points until, with Taylor back in his familiar defensive role, the ball clipped his foot and fell perfectly for Keith Downing to volley home with two minutes left.

'If the ball hadn't hit Shaun, it would have gone 40 yards wide, and we would have won the game 2-1,' declared Micky Hazard afterwards. Maskell had opened his Town account 15 minutes in, and seven days later he claimed his first hat-trick.

Games with Cambridge United had become almost synonymous with the clash of Hoddle's footballing philosophies and opposing manager John Beck's more fundamental tactics, and this one was to be no different.

Hoddle couldn't hide his disapproval of the physical methods deployed by Beck's side and seemed to take the win as a personal vindication of his own beliefs of the way the game should be played. The 34-year-old ran the game at the County Ground, supplying the cross for Taylor to power home a typical header 12 minutes in before Craig Maskell took over the goalscoring duties.

Not that there weren't plenty of opportunities for the list of scorers to be swelled with other names.

Bodin was the chief offender, seeing a penalty saved but forcing another good save from John Vaughan, but Maskell capitalised on a fumble from the custodian before half-time to double the lead.

Hoddle's side then turned the screw with Ling and Moncur both firing off target. Maskell added his second as the encounter became somewhat of an exhibition of contrasting styles. Swindon started to showboat with over-extravagant passing moves, nutmegs and back-heels, something that was bound to antagonise the opposition who responded with some nasty, over-vigorous challenges.

When Maskell despatched Town's fourth from the penalty spot to complete his hat-trick with little over 15 minutes remaining, the game was effectively well over. An 88th-minute goal for the visitors went barely noticed.

The previous season's dark horse promotion challengers were left bottom of the table without a point after four matches. Meanwhile, Swindon had completed August unbeaten and collected ten points from 12, scoring four times in a match twice and sitting second behind Charlton Athletic.

Things were looking good for a promotion push. Well, at least until September started.

Despite Maskell's opening goal at The Den, a 2-1 loss against Millwall inflicted the first defeat of the campaign five days into the month. Then the visit of Bristol Rovers to the County Ground, just over three weeks since the reverse fixture, was the first of a pair of home local derby matches for Hoddle's men.

The Gas looked cooked with four minutes remaining. Dave Mitchell had opened the scoring halfway through the first half, Marcus Stewart equalised with a penalty on 69 minutes, only for Maskell to score his fifth in five matches to restore Town's lead.

But when John Taylor levelled in the 86th minute it was the fifth consecutive time that Swindon had conceded in the last five minutes of a match, and an inquest was about to start in the changing room.

'We have to put it right and stop conceding goals in the last five minutes. We are fit enough, usually in control of matches, playing excellent football, creating chances and scoring some great goals, but the points are slipping away at the death,' was Hoddle's accurate assessment.

Assistant manager John Gorman added, 'I was screaming at the lads to make them aware that it was the last five minutes and to keep it tight, but the same thing has happened again.'

Over those five matches, late goals conceded had cost Swindon five points. And it happened again on TV the following Sunday, when Oxford United visited Wiltshire and claimed a share of the points with a goal six minutes from time.

Town led twice, through Ling and Taylor, but again surrendered maximum points with the second 2-2 draw in successive home matches. Local pride had been damaged twice in eight days.

When the Robins travelled to second-placed Charlton Athletic in the last week of September, they were facing the team with the meanest defence in the country, the Addicks having conceded just two goals in eight matches. Town were generally scoring, but if that dried up the defence was proving too insecure to protect a clean sheet.

Whether Hoddle's instructions to tighten up in the last minutes of the game had been misinterpreted is not known.

But following the boss's directions, this time Town conceded a whole 12 minutes before the end, which could have been considered an improvement.

Added to an 11th-minute strike, Charlton claimed a 2-0 win and Swindon had concluded the first match of the season in which they hadn't scored. They dropped to eighth in the table.

While August had been completed undefeated, September looked like ending without a win.

Respite from dropped league points came with a 6-0 away win over Torquay United of the bottom tier in the League Cup. Five different scorers and a clean sheet did something to rebuild belief, but in truth the gap in status should probably have indicated such an outcome was always a possibility.

The Gulls featured Paul Trollope, who had been given a free transfer from the County Ground in the summer without making a league appearance. He was on course to rebuild from the disappointment of release from the club where his father John, as great a legend as Swindon Town have ever had, was still youth team manager, with Paul on his way to later gaining nine Welsh caps.

When the second leg ended in a 3-2 win, Town were more than safely through to round three, but a 1-0 home defeat at the hands of Oldham Athletic stopped that potential Wembley route.

Back in league action, the penultimate day of September brought a visit of Grimsby Town, and at last three points. A second-minute Maskell goal secured a 1-0 win against the Mariners and took Town up to fifth. It was Maskell's seventh league strike of the season with nine games played.

Three days into October he was at it again. A Maskell brace against Watford at the County Ground, added to a trademark diving header by Taylor three minutes from time, saw the Robins claim a 3-1 victory and consecutive wins for the first time since the opening week of the season.

Over the next four weeks, Swindon were to do their promotion hopes no harm at all.

Despite a 3-1 reverse inflicted by Portsmouth at Fratton Park, a game in which ex-Swindon favourite Alan McLoughlin scored for the home side, all three of the remaining matches of the month were won.

Five goals from five different scorers did for Notts County on 17 October. By this point Nicky Hammond had reclaimed the number one jersey but was unable to prevent a 55th-minute goal for the visitors, by which time Swindon were already three goals to the good. Then Maskell got back in on the act, his 84th-minute effort claiming the only goal of the match at Upton Park against West Ham United, before converting a fourth-minute penalty at home to Barnsley on Halloween to bring another 1-0 win.

Throughout September the Robins had taken just five points from five games, a run which had damaged August's excellent start of ten points from the available 12. But in October the 12 from 15 had restored both belief and league position.

The win against Barnsley secured second place in the table, already five points behind leaders and eventual champions Newcastle United, but three ahead of third-placed Leicester City.

What was needed next was for the good points return to continue into November, rather than slip away as it had done at the turn of previous calendar months.

A settled squad would be ideal in furthering these aims.

But mid-October had seen Micky Hazard reject a £130,000 move to Sunderland, a deal which had surprisingly been agreed between the two clubs when Glenn Hoddle had indicated he could leave. The 32-year-old Sunderland-born-and-bred midfielder told the local press, 'I honestly thought I would be finishing my career at Swindon because I am very happy here. It came as a shock to me that they had accepted the offer. It obviously means I am dispensable. My two years here have been extremely happy, and I have never had a reason to want to leave.'

Hazard had been virtually ever-present during the season so far and the proposed move had come as a surprise to the player himself and supporters, who were left wondering whether there were any off-field reasons for the events. Hoddle himself had denied any rift between his player and the club.

The answer came three days before the end of October, and it came as little surprise. 'Swindon £2.5m in debt' sang the *Evening Advertiser*'s headline as the club's annual accounts were released.

The previous year's £500,000 profit had descended to a £1.3m loss. Board members were increasing their financial exposure to the club, £200,000 expected from Manchester City for appearance-related income from the sale of Fitzroy Simpson seemed to have already been swallowed up, and £125,000 due to Reading for the recruitment of Craig Maskell had still not been accounted for in the outgoing column.

Unsurprisingly, recently mooted ideas of a move to a purpose-built new stadium were abandoned in favour of a redevelopment of the existing County Ground.

The reason for the bad fiscal news was given as a decrease in the income from transfer fees, giving every indication that an annual seven-figure player sale had become perceived as an accounting necessity, rather than a bonus.

The sale of top scorer Duncan Shearer had scuppered the previous season's promotion hopes. The loss of Alan McLoughlin the year before had also done untold damage. Meanwhile, new top scorer Craig Maskell had scored six times in the last seven matches. Town supporters held their breath.

Another year, another financial horror story. What now for on-field confidence?

The swift answer to that was a 2-0 Tuesday evening home loss to Brentford. Just how much the mood on the pitch was affected by the financial position could only be guessed at, but pre-match, Brentford were only two points clear of the relegation zone. It was only the second time Town had failed to score in 15 matches, and another month had started when results were not to be reflective of those of the previous one.

Another goalless encounter, this one at Newcastle, brought a point from a very creditable 0-0 draw as Town failed to score again, and two more away draws at Bristol City and Peterborough massaged self-respect but saw the cushion between second and third continually eroded.

In between, a 3-2 home win over Southend United brought Swindon's only win of November, with the month closing as the Robins were overhauled by Tranmere Rovers in the table. The difference between second and third at the end of the season would be automatic promotion to the Premier League, or the all-or-nothing drama of the play-offs.

With Nicky Hammond now safely in control of the goalkeeper's jersey, a strange opportunity had opened up for Fraser Digby in November, certainly one that would prove impossible for the ex-Manchester United man to turn down. Alex Ferguson came calling and requested that Digby took a temporary sabbatical back at Old Trafford covering a goalkeeping injury crisis. So it was that Town's second-choice keeper was to spend two months readying himself on the United bench to replace Peter Schmeichel at a moment's notice.

December didn't bring a great deal of cheer on the pitch or opportunity to regain ground in the table. Only two games were completed and each brought thumping defeats.

A match against Derby County on a deteriorating County Ground pitch brought a sixth successive away victory for the Rams as Swindon had no answer to the pace of the visitors' forward play. Hazard and Maskell grabbed goals in the last three minutes, but that was no match for the four the Rams had already raided.

Maskell's goal was his 18th of the season, and when left-back Kevin Horlock was unceremoniously downed in the penalty box seconds later it was Maskell who spurned the opportunity for number 19 by allowing Derby keeper Steve Sutton to complete an impressive display with a face-saving penalty stop in a breathless finish.

The weather was to intervene through December, and it was a whole two weeks later that Town travelled to Filbert Street for their next match. Having already lost 4-2 to Derby, they couldn't prevent it happening once more against Leicester City. And this time the result was compounded with the sending-off of Colin Calderwood for two bookable offences.

The day brought criticism for Hoddle who for the second game chose to play himself in midfield rather than his traditional sweeper role, with his defence reverting to a flat back four. That resulted in the second 4-2 defeat in December, not the sort of impact that his tactical decision-making would have intended.

That there had only been one other fixture attempted in December was also due to a floodlight failure at the County Ground 51 minutes into the match against Tranmere. John Aldridge had already struck twice to give Rovers a two-goal, half-time lead, and as the Saturday afternoon, winter light faded, Ling reduced the arrears.

Rovers would have felt the greatest sense of injustice when the lights went out a minute later, but conversely Town's tails had been up with plenty of time left on the clock and perhaps had their own reasons to feel aggrieved.

The Christmas fixture fiesta also fell victim to the seasonal weather, with a scheduled Boxing Day trip to Luton and the 29 December visit of Birmingham City both needing rearrangements.

And in a pre-Christmas flash of foresight, a national newspaper article quoted England goalscoring legend Jimmy Greaves as proclaiming his belief that Glenn Hoddle would one day manage Tottenham Hotspur, the team which both had graced so influentially in the past. Greaves also speculated Hoddle's services could be requested to replace Graham Taylor as England manager. The speculation was not unique to Greaves, but would prove to be succinctly accurate.

The new year dawned and with it a televised Monday night FA Cup third round tie away at Premier League Queens Park Rangers, whose front line featured an up-and-coming forward called Les Ferdinand. Striker Dave

Mitchell occupied an unaccustomed role in the centre of Town's defence to cover for the suspended Colin Calderwood and for the first 20 minutes everything went as well as could have been expected.

Then Ferdinand decided to show his credentials and within the space of two first-half minutes, Swindon were two goals down. The future England man planted two almost identical downward headers past Hammond and that seemed to be that.

Three minutes after Ferdinand's second, Gary Penrice added Rangers' third and the job was done. The home team, who featured future Town figures Alan McDonald and Ian Holloway, were through to round four and Swindon's FA Cup campaign, such as it was, was over.

Financially strapped Swindon, eliminated from the League Cup back in October, had now been denied the income from an FA Cup run too.

So, with all the previous despondency brought about by the unveiling of the club accounts, it seemed a strange time to announce yet more new plans regarding the redevelopment of the Shrivenham Road side of the County Ground.

But there was method behind the apparent madness. A 16 January deadline needed to be beaten in order that the Robins qualified for a Football Trust grant towards the work. The project was predicted to cost between £1m and £1.5m, and the grant could contribute up to 75 per cent of the bill. As welcome as that was, for the rebuilding to go ahead still meant Swindon needed to find approaching £400,000.

Viewed another way, that looked like yet another significant player departure just as, yet again, Town were preparing for an assault on promotion to the top division.

Those supporters old enough to remember may well have been drawing comparisons to the early 1970s. Then the most famous Swindon player of all, Don Rogers, had departed for Crystal Palace for almost £150,000, with the incoming cheque generally considered the investment which allowed the building of the North Stand, opposite the newly mooted Shrivenham Road development.

Chairman Ray Hardman moved to quell concerns by saying, 'There are various ways of raising money for the project, but I do not want to sell players to build a new stand. That is not the way forward in my opinion.'

That the proposed South Stand revamp was well overdue could not be disputed. The seated upper tier of the vintage stand had been closed since the tragic Bradford City fire back in 1985, and restrictions on the lower terracing meant that that entire side of the ground was licensed to hold just 2,630 standing supporters.

If the finance could be secured, the loss of the old Aldershot tattoo-sourced facility would be mourned by few. But at what cost on the field?

Back on that field, the first league fixture of 1993 brought celebrations among Swindon fans as their side travelled the few short miles to Oxford and returned with three points and local pride. A Steve White goal secured a 1-0 win at the Manor Ground.

Scoring in the 34th minute in the week of his 34th birthday, the veteran striker, who had spent most of the campaign on the bench, made his first league start and grabbed his first goal in three months. It was the Robins' first win since mid-November and finally the seesawing of the results of alternate calendar months was about to end.

A new year and a win over their bitter local rivals; the next five months were to be the biggest in Swindon Town's history.

Successive home draws didn't necessarily suggest such. A midweek goalless encounter on a muddy pitch in front of almost 14,500 supporters saw the points shared when Birmingham City came to town. The Blues were just two points off the relegation zone and defended to leave with what they had when they arrived. Craig Maskell hit a post but that was as good as it got.

Glenn Hoddle proclaimed, 'We've thrown two points away. It was a tough game played in tough conditions. They came for a draw and got it. I could not fault our effort; we just needed a break to turn the game.'

The season was exactly halfway through, and the return fixture was scheduled for April. That one would live far longer in the memory.

Charlton Athletic were next, four days later. The early league leaders had plummeted to three points and three places behind seventh-placed Swindon. An early goal from ex-Robin Garry Nelson gave the visitors the lead, which was doubled on the half hour.

But by the time the half-time whistle blew, Nicky Summerbee, in an unfamiliar wide midfield role, netted from White's persistence in winning a loose ball and squaring to the youngster. Then a Bodin set piece supplied the chance for Calderwood to head home and square things up; it was to stay 2-2.

Summerbee's forward position had been enforced when Hoddle pulled a thigh muscle in the warm-up and the tried and trusted sweeper system had to be ditched. Any long-term absence of the influential boss and playmaker would be less than ideal. Thankfully those fears would be allayed, but further speculation muddied the waters on 25 January.

Bristol City's dismissal of manager Denis Smith had brought covetous glances at Hoddle from Ashton Gate. Ray Hardman astutely and ultimately correctly suggested, 'Glenn is under contract here for at least another year and we will do everything we can to keep him here. If anything does eventually force Glenn out of Swindon it is likely to be one of the bigger clubs who can offer him a massive salary and millions to spend.'

A reassuring statement from the top, but it would prove to be a prophetic one.

January entered its last week with Swindon standing two points and one place outside the play-off zone. A trip to Blundell Park lay ahead to face Grimsby Town, who had their own reason to climb the table. A win would hoist the Mariners within sight of the top six, and they weren't about to allow respect for Hoddle's reputation to cloud their own ambitions.

A 2-1 win for the home side took Grimsby to within a point of their Wiltshire visitors but would prove to be important for Swindon in two ways.

Firstly, Hoddle had shaken off his thigh injury and would miss just three more matches to the end of the season. Secondly, left-back Bodin scored the first of four goals in consecutive matches, polishing his scoring boots in readiness for what might be considered the most important penalty in Swindon's history.

There were 21 matches of the regular season to run, and Swindon were getting ready to right what was perceived as the greatest injustice ever inflicted on their club.

What followed were three consecutive victories, made possible with three clean sheets. Bodin secured a home win over Wolves with a 69th-minute far-post header from a Ling cross, which brought the only goal of the last game of the month.

A week later, a 1-0 win at Sunderland was achieved by Bodin's goal in the 53rd minute, which was again due to consummate teamwork between the same two men. Bodin first made an interception and brought Ling into play as the full-back charged on an overlapping run. When Ling returned the ball to the marauding Welsh international, Bodin's strike left Tony Norman in the Sunderland goal helpless.

The man known as Zippy was showing plenty of zip, but the outcome was not the result of a one-man show. Fraser Digby, who had returned from his Old Trafford adventure to reclaim the number one shirt from the injured Nicky Hammond, had earlier pushed a 13th-minute Gordon Armstrong penalty on to the post; the game was into injury time when referee Kevin Lynch awarded Sunderland the second penalty of the match. This time Kevin Ball troubled the advertising hoardings rather than Digby's goal and the points were on their way south to Wiltshire.

The Robins made it nine points from nine with a 3-0 home victory over Millwall on 13 February. With the goals spread so well among the team, the last time a Swindon striker had hit the back of the net had been in the first game of the year when Steve White had clinched the win at Oxford.

And it was White again who took until the last minute of the first half to open the scoring against the Lions, rounding his marker and finishing clinically past goalkeeper Kasey Keller.

Then Bodin was at it again 15 minutes into the second half. Ling was once more a major contributor, dummying cleverly to allow a Summerbee ball to reach Bodin, whose precise drive cannoned into the net off a post.

But the architect of the win was undoubtedly player-boss Hoddle, who ran the show in the way that only he could, spraying passes and organising Swindon's afternoon's work against the team who sat third in the table.

Trying his luck with an impudent 35-yard free kick, Hoddle almost caught Keller out at his near post, and seven minutes from the end he produced the skilful flick which allowed centre-back Shaun Taylor to blast home his ninth goal of the season.

Swindon were back in the play-off places and there were 18 games to play. Things seemed to be going too well. Plainly a reality check was in order.

The headline 'Hard-up Swindon's Cash Crisis Grows' seemed to fit the bill. 'We need a fairy godmother says chairman Ray Hardman' came the strapline. The *Evening Advertiser* was as used to writing the headlines as the supporters were used to reading them.

Reported as losing £12,000 every home game, there was apparently no money available to strengthen the team and, despite again being in a position to push for promotion to the Premier League, selling players could not be ruled out.

While the news seemed oh so familiar, one statement seemed to quantify the problem starkly. 'We need crowds of 13,000 to 14,000 every week to break even,' said Hardman.

With the average attendance standing at around 8,000, Hardman was mentioning figures not seen regularly at the County Ground since 1972.

Whether the difference between need and reality had come about through financial mismanagement, over-ambition, or indifference among the Swindon public was a matter for debate. What seemed clear was that Town's best chance of breaking even was to reach the Premier League in the shortest time possible but that, paradoxically, trying to do so would continue to expose the club to the greatest risk of financial failure.

A 1-0 defeat at Cambridge on 20 February didn't help, but the windy conditions and difficult pitch gave Hoddle's side opportunities for excuses. A 76th-minute penalty sealed the points for the U's as the Robins' run of three consecutive wins was surrendered.

On the Tuesday three days later, the Tranmere fans who made the trip back to Wiltshire after December's floodlight-induced abandonment showed their humour and readiness for the occasion by arriving with torches to mitigate against a reoccurrence. But it was not through a shortage of illumination that Rovers goalkeeper Eric Nixon couldn't see a way to prevent Dave Mitchell scoring twice.

The first came after ten minutes when a combination of White and Ling ended with Ling's snap strike being too hot for Nixon to hold, with Mitchell pouncing to net the loose ball. Then Hoddle, who was again controlling the game, claimed a ball in midfield and played an exquisite, scooped pass which took the entire Tranmere defence out of the game. Mitchell, anticipating just what his boss was capable of, accelerated past the static defence, controlled the ball on his chest and beat Nixon for a second time.

Tranmere, who had started the evening a point ahead of Swindon, were overhauled courtesy of Town's 2-0 victory which moved them to fifth in the table.

There was one last game in February to play, when the Robins went one better at home to Portsmouth. Bodin's 88th-minute strike grabbed all three points for Town's second consecutive victory, and the win this time meant they leapfrogged Pompey up to fourth.

But when Swindon visited Vicarage Road to take on mid-table Watford on 6 March, belief was elevated even higher, both in terms of league position and performance.

Steve White hit his first hat-trick in almost six years as Town ran riot. White struck his first just two minutes in, pouncing on a loose ball when Mitchell's strong header was spilled by home keeper Perry Suckling.

His second, and Town's third, came on the half hour after a Taylor header thumped against the bar, Calderwood returning the ball to the far post and White beating his marker to nod home.

Nine minutes from time, Hoddle's glorious free kick found a running Bodin, whose cross was perfectly placed for White to volley home beautifully and complete his hat-trick.

Mitchell's 21st-minute goal, while understandably overshadowed by his strike partner's exploits, again demonstrated the artistry that Hoddle's team were capable of. Ross MacLaren's ball to Bodin saw the left-back produce another wonderful centre for the Australian international to bury his header past Suckling.

The 4-0 away win meant that Swindon were now just one place off the top two, although in truth the seven-point difference between third-placed Town and second-placed West Ham looked unbridgeable. Perhaps eyeing a more realistic likelihood, the same points difference separated Swindon from seventh-placed Leicester, the team occupying the position just outside the play-off zone.

Despite the ongoing off-field financial stories, Hoddle's team were concentrating on their football magnificently. Six of the last seven games had been won, 12 goals had been scored and just one conceded. And they were to lose just twice more before May. There were 14 games left to the end of the season and Swindon looked as if they were timing their run for the play-offs perfectly.

Hoddle said in the Portsmouth programme, 'There is no lack of ambition at this club. There is no shadow of a doubt that if the board had the money they would invest in our future. Our position is not unique. An extra two or three thousand on the gate could alleviate the need to sell players to survive.'

And as if to demonstrate the potential, over 14,000 had turned up to see Town put Pompey to the sword 1-0, although the travelling south coast hordes would have significantly swelled the number.

Six of the remaining matches were at home, with some big-name opposition among them. Three would meet Hardman's attendance target. Would that be enough to keep the transfer wolves from the door?

Within days the answer to that was forthcoming.

'Fans erupt over the sale of Kerslake' was the *Advertiser*'s assessment. First Division champions Leeds United had put forward £500,000 to take full-back David, who had been ever present in the first team since August, to Elland Road.

Not only that, but it was also understood that Hoddle and Gorman were ready to quit the County Ground should there be any further departures before the transfer deadline passed.

'It's something I didn't want, but the board said it had to be done,' said Hoddle regarding the Kerslake sale. 'We have put ourselves into such a good position to reach the Premier League, which would solve a lot of our financial problems. In my mind there will not be any more players sold.'

That last comment sounded like a challenge to the board, and a thinly disguised threat should it happen.

With Crystal Palace rumoured to be casting envious eyes at Colin Calderwood, the atmosphere was tinder dry with everyone fearing a calamitous spark.

A midweek 1-1 draw at relegation-threatened Southend United settled nerves, a 68th-minute Steve White equaliser levelling four minutes after the home side had taken the lead. Nicky Summerbee moved back to cover the departed Kerslake, and Adi Viveash made his first appearance of the season as suddenly Hoddle was absent from the team. A conspiracist would have had a field day.

Viveash was to keep his place for four matches, and the next one up was against league leaders Newcastle at home.

An attendance of 17,574 would have pleased chairman Ray Hardman, and the 2-1 win delighted everyone who considered Wiltshire rather than Tyneside their home.

Losing 1-0 at half-time, Paul Bodin's 51st-minute penalty after a White tumble and Calderwood's vital six-yard touch four minutes later inflicted defeat on Kevin Keegan's side, keeping Swindon third in the table.

A midweek goalless draw at Luton gave way to another big encounter with a televised trip to the Baseball Ground to take on Derby.

Hoddle named himself among the substitutes and replaced Viveash with 15 minutes remaining, but the afternoon ended in Swindon's first defeat in two months. Town had dominated throughout but had been undone in a five-minute period in the second half. Shaun Taylor's tenth goal of the season in the 72nd minute counted for nothing as the Rams, booed off at half-time, completed a league double over the Robins with a 2-1 win.

The outcome of the four-match cameo for Viveash could have been considered harsh on the Wootton Bassett-born defender. He had been overlooked all season, then while understudying an ex-England legend he had remained in an undefeated team until his boss returned to the field, and was discarded again until May.

The March transfer deadline had passed without further incident. PFA chairman and ex-England international Brian Marwood had arrived the month before from Sheffield United, and he was having a positive effect on the field, taking over wide-man responsibilities with Summerbee at full-back.

Marwood was to strike his only goal for Town in the next match, at home to Bristol City, a win that dropped the Ashton Gate side into the relegation zone.

Marwood's diving header opened the scoring inside 20 minutes, Bodin added a successful penalty, and Leroy Rosenior's late consolation for City never seriously threatened to change the destination of the points. Town had won six home matches on the trot and sat a comfortable-looking nine points inside the play-off zone.

The last game of March brought a trip to Brentford, at the time still playing at Griffin Park and struggling to stay outside the relegation zone. Swindon had faced more threatening-looking opposition, but this was to be no ordinary afternoon. And the problems could be considered either self-inflicted or dictated by referee Vic Callow.

Both sides had chances, but in the 32nd minute the game took its first twist. White challenged Keith Millen to an aerial ball launched by Digby, as an elbow struck the Bees defender's head and Callow produced a red card for White.

Four minutes later Mitchell chased down Millen, clipped his ankle and Callow was in his pocket again for a yellow for Mitchell. Then with just two minutes of the first half remaining, Mitchell left his studs up in yet another challenge with Millen. Callow sprang into action again and waved a red card in the direction of the striker.

Hoddle was furious with Mitchell for needlessly, and badly, challenging a worthless ball, and Swindon were to face the entire second half without either of their first-choice frontmen. White's recollection of the afternoon on which he received the only red card of his career can be found later in the book.

Forty-five minutes of desperate defending followed as Town, without an out-ball option available, clung on to the goalless scoreline. With seconds left Ling won a ball on the edge of Town's box and ran towards the halfway line. Squaring to Hoddle, the boss found substitute Shaun Close running into space, whose persistence allowed him to pick out the charging Bodin.

But one-on-one with goalkeeper Graham Benstead, Bodin's strike at goal sailed agonisingly over the crossbar as the Robins came desperately close to snatching an unlikely and heroic three points.

The two points dropped left Town fourth in the table. Had Bodin's effort been on target, all three would have found their way to Wiltshire and Swindon would have been just two points off an automatic promotion place.

As April commenced, Newcastle looked secure at the top with a five-point cushion above upwardly mobile Portsmouth. West Ham had dropped to third, with Leicester and Millwall below Swindon making up the rest of the play-off zone places.

A six-point gap existed between sixth-placed Millwall and Tranmere in seventh, while there were a further four points between Rovers and eighth-placed Wolverhampton Wanderers. The campaign was entering its closing straight and it was beginning to look like the play-offs would comprise any four from six.

There were six matches for Hoddle's men to play in April. Only one would be lost, and one would produce a scoreline that would defy all explanation.

The first saw mid-table Peterborough United welcomed to a wet and windy County Ground, three points gained and the deadly Bodin once again sealing the outcome with his eighth goal in 14 appearances. Not only that – four of the strikes had now come in otherwise goalless games, turning expected single-point returns into three.

His 67th minute strike to beat the Posh came from a typical dummy and pass from his boss. The classic Hoddle manoeuvre allowed Bodin the space to canter into the visitors' penalty box and leave keeper Ian Bennett helpless from 15 yards.

The scoreline didn't reflect Swindon's dominance, with Marwood shooting narrowly wide from 20 yards and Taylor missing the target from six. Before the end Summerbee had hit the side-netting, Mitchell had struck the bar, and Digby had barely been called into action.

The Robins' point haul stood at 68 for the season, and it could be argued that eight of them had come as a direct result of four goals from Bodin. And his most important goal of all was less than two months away.

On 6 April Swindon travelled to Tranmere for a midweek fixture that looked crucial for both teams. Rovers sat one place but four points outside the play-off places, desperately eyeing the points to close the gap. Meanwhile, if Swindon were to mount one last challenge for automatic promotion, the earlier the better.

When Mitchell opened the scoring halfway through the first half, things looked good for Hoddle's objectives. Depending on stout defending and quick raiding attacks, White – in his final appearance before a suspension – had capitalised on a clumsy Tranmere defensive mistake to arrow in on keeper Eric Nixon, draw him out of goal then square the ball to Mitchell for a simple finish.

Digby responded manfully to several goal-bound attempts, but the first half was seen out with Town still in the driving seat.

But then the game turned into the Kenny Irons show as Tranmere's midfielder cracked in a hat-trick to boost the home side's promotion hopes; it finished 3-1 in the second encounter of the season between the two sides. They were destined to meet twice more in little over a month, by which time league positions would be insignificant.

Luton Town's trip to the County Ground on Easter Saturday four days later brought the first league start of the season for Shaun Close, as the Robins took to the field without their regular strikers, both suspended. Luckily, Craig Maskell, after two months out with a hamstring problem, had battled his way back to bolster the front line.

The resulting win, however, was courtesy of one of so many single-goal victories that season. With seven minutes left, Bodin latched on to a flick from debutant substitute Chris Hamon, on the pitch for just a minute, to bury the only strike of the match.

The promotion push was still on with five games to go, although the five-point gap to the automatic promotion places meant the play-offs were surely the most likely route for Hoddle's team to gain promotion to the Premier League.

Then on Easter Monday came a trip to St Andrew's to face Birmingham City. The Blues were not having the best of seasons, struggling just a win's worth of points away from the relegation zone, but this looked a significantly more difficult task than against Luton. This game would still be talked about decades later.

'Shell-shocked,' was Hoddle's assessment at the final whistle. 'Don't ask me to explain that one.'

It had started tamely enough, taking 25 minutes before a slip by Ross MacLaren allowed Dean Peer to open the scoring for the home side. Four minutes later, Birmingham broke from a Swindon corner for John Frain to add a second. But between those two goals, an unfortunate clash of heads had seen Shaun Taylor leave the field to receive ten stitches to a gash above his left eye, leaving Swindon with ten men for seven minutes.

Back on the field just before half-time, the patched-up Taylor announced his reintroduction and added to his growing cult status by powering home a header from a Micky Hazard free kick to make the score 2-1.

Three minutes into the second half Paul Moulden raced clear to increase City's lead, then Andy Saville fired home an unstoppable drive from 25 yards three minutes later. What now for Swindon's promotion push, 4-1 down with little over half the match played?

That's the way it stayed until an hour in when Hazard's ball found Maskell free in the box, the striker planting his low shot sweetly past Andy Gosney. Five minutes later,

Taylor, in an unusual position wide on the left of the Blues' penalty area, chipped a ball towards the six-yard box. Gosney pawed at the cross, lost it, and Mitchell nodded calmly into the exposed net.

There was then a brief hiatus for all of ten minutes, after which Ling collected a long ball and steered it back to Maskell, who squared to the incoming Mitchell to make the score 4-4.

Two minutes after that, rampant Town took the lead as a routine Bodin corner found Maskell, who looped a header under the bar for his second of the match.

Town's travelling supporters had been demanding referee John Lloyd's final whistle when Ling launched a long ball from his own half towards Mitchell. The striker out-paced and out-muscled Richard Dryden, left Gosney on the floor and completed his hat-trick: Birmingham City 4 Swindon Town 6.

With four games of the regular season still to play it would be difficult to follow such breathless action, and strangely it would prove to be unnecessary.

The following Saturday a 1-1 home draw with Leicester left both clubs where they had started. Neither retained any realistic ambitions of claiming an automatic promotion place, but sitting occupying fourth and fifth they would have felt relatively confident in securing a play-off berth.

Town in particular were eight points clear of seventh place with nine points to play for, and another 1-1 draw at Notts County meant that only an unlikely and drastic reduction in goal difference could prevent them from making the end-of-season bonanza.

Even consecutive losses to about-to-be-promoted West Ham and couldn't-care-less mid-table Barnsley saw

Swindon finish fifth on 76 points, level with Leicester in sixth. Tranmere were fourth on 79 and a disappointed Portsmouth finished level with West Ham on 88 points but missed out on automatic promotion courtesy of their inferior goalscoring record.

It ultimately transpired that if Swindon were to succeed in their quest to join the Premier League, they would have to overcome Tranmere and Leicester in the play-offs to achieve it. They had faced both in April – and hadn't beaten either one.

Eight days after the First Division season had finished for 20 of the 24 clubs, Tranmere visited the County Ground on a Sunday afternoon in front of the TV cameras for the first leg of the play-off semi-final.

John Moncur, without a start since December, was named in midfield with Hazard on the bench. The rest of Hoddle's team showed few surprises. Meanwhile, for the visitors, dangerous striker John Aldridge, unavailable when the teams met 40 days earlier, led the front line.

A good start was essential for both sides, but surely only possible for one.

Two minutes in, Rovers' 6ft 3in centre-back Steve Vickers beat Mitchell to a Summerbee near-post cross but only powered it past his own goalkeeper Eric Nixon. The travelling supporters in the 14,230 crowd had their heads in their hands, while the rest went ballistic.

Then less than a minute later, Vickers sloppily messed up a penalty box clearance and Ross MacLaren tried his luck from 25 yards, forcing Nixon to parry on his goal line. Charging forward in anticipation was Mitchell again, and he calmly slotted the ball past the keeper's despairing foot.

Three minutes in and Town were two goals to the good. Cue disbelieving jubilation from three sides of the ground, the members of whom plainly felt that this was, indeed, a good start.

Aldridge was then ruled to have pushed Hoddle as he headed what he thought was a goalscoring retort. The reprieve brought a sigh of relief from the Swindon contingent, and in the 26th minute the Robins' lead was increased further.

A long kick from Digby seemed to have been dealt with by Tranmere, but Maskell intercepted a pass, fed Mitchell and the Aussie international homed in on goal through an overcommitted defence.

Nixon came out to shut Mitchell down, but Maskell had continued his own run in support of his team-mate. Mitchell squared the ball to his fellow striker and it was 3-0.

Less than half an hour gone and there was a feeling that the back of the tie had been broken. Swindon's finishing had been ruthless, referee Allan Gunn's contribution had been helpful, and the question was whether the Robins should stick or twist.

That question seemed to be answered when early in the second half, Mitchell's header from a Hoddle free kick struck the crossbar and deflected to safety.

But Tranmere hadn't finished three points ahead of Swindon by accident. In the 58th minute John Morrissey collected the ball wide on the right, cut inside past Summerbee and curled a marvellous shot past Digby.

'I'm happy with that,' Hoddle told the TV cameras afterwards. 'I'm a little bit disappointed that we let them back in with a goal, but we performed extremely well in the first half. I didn't expect us to keep that tempo going for 90 minutes but it's nice to go up there with a two-goal lead.'

A reminder that the tie wasn't finished, and before the second leg on 19 May came the worry that Hoddle had aggravated a groin strain and MacLaren, named man of the match by the TV crew, was also doubtful.

Come Wednesday night, both men were declared fit, and the stage was set for the culmination of the season for one of the two teams; once again Swindon took the initiative.

John Moncur drew first blood almost half an hour in, firing home from the edge of the box after good work from Ling and Summerbee.

Three goals behind on aggregate, Tranmere's response seemed to be to launch high balls towards Aldridge, but they were met by a colossal performance from Taylor and an imperious display from Calderwood.

Digby produced a fine save as the first half drew to a close, but two minutes into added time Mark Proctor volleyed home a Pat Nevin cross.

Steve White failed to return after the interval as a recurring hamstring injury flared up, and five minutes into the second period Digby produced a vital stop, clawing the ball away as Rovers players claimed unsuccessfully that it had crossed the line.

Nevin failed to hit the target from three yards, but then netted with 25 minutes left as the ball appeared to have been kicked from the hands of the outstretched Digby; 2-1 on the night to Tranmere, 4-3 on aggregate to Swindon.

And it all seemed decided eight minutes from time when Mitchell forced an error from Vickers, who would have been cursing the day he had first heard Mitchell's name. His square ball to Maskell, on for the withdrawn White, was struck towards goal but the shot was blocked by Nixon and Maskell alertly stuck away the rebound.

There was still time for Hoddle to uncharacteristically foul Morrissey in the box and Irons to make the aggregate score 5-4 from the penalty spot, and then an eternity for the travelling fans to wait for Paul Durkin to blow his final whistle. Swindon Town had reached Wembley.

'It felt like the longest six minutes of my life,' said assistant boss John Gorman about the added time. 'To think I got the goal that took us to Wembley is a dream come true,' declared Maskell. 'Seven years ago, I was not even a pro,' pontificated Shaun Taylor, who had come into the Football League from Bideford Town.

Fraser Digby had a thought for past events and a ghost to be laid to rest, 'It meant so much more after the disappointment of 1990. We felt we had to win – for the players who missed out last time and most of all for the fans. I just want one more win to put us back up where we belong.'

There were thousands of supporters who were ready to drink to that.

And Glenn Hoddle declared, 'I've known from day one the sense of injustice felt by our supporters over what happened three years ago. I want them to know we are doing this for them as much as for ourselves.'

So to 31 May, a bank holiday Monday.

Leicester had successfully overcome third-placed Portsmouth and stood in the way of Hoddle's side with the Premier League the destination for the winners.

Dave Mitchell faced a dilemma which might have seen him called up by Australia to face New Zealand in a World Cup qualifier. That worry was put to bed when manager Eddie Thompson allowed the 34-cap Mitchell to remain on club duties.

Fellow striker Steve White declared his hopes of shaking off the hamstring strain that had forced him off at Tranmere.

'Win it for the fans says Ossie' was the headline in the *Evening Advertiser*, as ex-boss Ardiles conveyed his best wishes to Hoddle's team. 'I want justice for Swindon says Lou' came the following night, Lou Macari passing on his own message of support.

'I would like to wish them all the best. They are certainly good enough for the Premier League,' said Duncan Shearer. 'The fans are the ones I feel most for. They were cheated last time.'

Ex-Town defender David Hockaday said, 'I'm confident Swindon are going to make it into the Premier League and get some justice for what happened three years ago.'

Tension was building and 35,000 Swindon fans were preparing to relocate to Wembley on the last day of the month. The word 'justice' was not far from the lips of any of them either. Perhaps unexpectedly for a bank holiday Monday on the last day of spring, the day broke bright, dry and warm. Just the sort of day for history to be made.

Town lined up against Leicester in familiar style. Digby was between the posts, the defensive flanks were manned by Summerbee and Bodin, with Calderwood and Taylor between them. Hoddle took his usual place, patrolling in front of or behind the back four depending on where he could use his skills most effectively and switching with MacLaren as dictated. Moncur and Ling completed the midfield, and with White still suffering a hamstring pull, the front two were Maskell and Mitchell. Hazard completed the 13-man matchday squad, on the bench with White.

Leicester, who had been defeated by Blackburn at the same stage the previous season, had qualified for this final by beating Portsmouth 3-2 on aggregate. Julian Joachim and Steve Thompson had both scored and were named in the Wembley line-up, while the third semi-final scorer, Ian Ormondroyd, was on the bench.

Nip and tuck followed the first whistle, with both teams testing the Wembley water. Summerbee fired over some right-wing crosses towards Mitchell and Maskell to try out Foxes keeper Kevin Poole's handling, while Leicester's Gary Mills and Steve Thompson tried their luck from distance, but half-time was on the horizon without either team showing evidence of what was to come.

Ten minutes before the break, Bodin's near-post corner was flicked on by Hoddle, but City defender Richard Smith made an important interception to prevent Mitchell's intended strike at goal. Then at the other end, Digby just beat Joachim to a Steve Walsh cross, before making another stop from David Oldfield's goal-bound shot.

But the game took its most significant turn so far with three minutes of the first half remaining.

Ling, later to be named man of the match by the TV commentary team, brought Moncur into play, with the ball switched to the opposite wing to Summerbee on the right. His cross was expertly controlled by Maskell, who held up play awaiting the arrival of his boss. Maskell's marvellous back-heel to the approaching Hoddle gave him all the opportunity he needed to curl a 20-yard shot past Poole to open the scoring.

The half-time team talks for both sides would surely be changed, but it's unlikely that Leicester City's boss Brian Little would have told his team, 'Now go out and concede two more.'

Just two minutes after the restart, Maskell netted his 24th of the season. Moncur's exquisite footwork took five

City defenders out of the game before he re-fed his team-mate, whose left-footed finish clattered off Poole's far post to double Town's lead.

Seven minutes later, Summerbee's corner from the right scythed through the celebratory toilet roll still littering the pitch towards Shaun Taylor's head. The ball was headed clear as far as Moncur, who headed it back into the danger area as the City defenders were still trying to evacuate their penalty box.

Taylor, still onside, saw the ball falling to him and heroically stuck his head where the lunging Poole was trying to claim it. There was only to be one winner, the courageous centre-back braving the approaching fists of the goalkeeper to nod Swindon into a three-goal lead.

The game was 54 minutes old, Swindon appeared to hold an unassailable advantage and pandemonium was ensuing in one half of Wembley.

However, three minutes later, Leicester broke from defence and skilfully engineered an attack down Swindon's right. Lee Philpott fired over a cross, Walsh headed against Digby's left-hand post and Joachim crashed home the loose ball on the six-yard line.

Eleven minutes further on, several opportunities were missed to deal with a Foxes attack. Mills crossed to the far post, Philpott hooked it whence it came, and Walsh was allowed to nod home Leicester's second of the match.

Shell-shocked Swindon had no time to regroup and a further 60 seconds passed before City's Mike Whitlow broke and found Steve Thompson, who had the freedom of the centre of Town's defence to run through and slide the ball under the diving Digby.

Swindon had scored three goals in 12 minutes and conceded three in 13.

Digby and Calderwood were both pressed into action to stop the turnaround turning into disaster but slowly footballing normality started to return. And with it, the formal casting of two Swindon Town footballing legends into immortality. With 11 minutes of normal time remaining, the veteran Steve White stepped off the bench to replace Maskell.

First, Ling produced a desperate save from Poole as Swindon tried once again to reassert their superiority, then Moncur brought Hoddle into the game, and his long ball was hoisted toward the charging White.

The 34-year-old arrowed in on goal just as Poole charged out to shut down the danger. Poole went to punch clear ahead of the lunging White, careered into the striker and clattered him to the ground.

Referee David Elleray, so far an inconspicuous contributor to the game, pointed to the spot and Paul Bodin had the chance to enter Robins history.

Five minutes from the end of normal time, and with extra time on everybody's mind, the Welsh international stepped up, blasted the ball to his right, past the wrong-way-diving Poole, and Swindon were soon to become a Premier League club.

Over 16 appearances in 1993, Bodin had scored the only goal of the game five times. In doing so he had converted five draws into five wins, and without those extra ten points Swindon would have finished the season in eighth, missing out on the play-offs. And without Bodin scoring the very last goal of the season, five minutes from the very end of the final match, they would never have reached the Premier League.

Meanwhile, Town supporters were consulting their still-to-be-invented smartphones to check on the newly invented internet whether they could lobby mid-term Pope John Paul II to canonise new hero Hoddle for leading their team to the recently inaugurated Premier League.

If this was the direction of the future, fans couldn't wait to climb aboard the pie-in-the-sky HS2. Cheers, Saint Glenn.

In the aftermath, Colin Calderwood commented, 'I feel very proud to have skippered this side. This win means a lot to me having captained the side through all the divisions.'

Bodin said, 'The lap of honour brought home just how much it means to the town. The way it was taken away three years ago was disgusting. I'm just pleased I've helped put that all in the past.'

Taylor added, 'What more is there to do? I've played at Wembley, scored a goal and finished up in the Premier League.'

Maskell said, 'It's a dream come true. To score a goal on my first trip here and win promotion is almost unthinkable.'

White was disappointed not to have started but said, 'I was absolutely delighted to get on the pitch and show what I could do. That led to my room-mate "Baldrick" Bodin scoring the winner!'

Most of the 35,000 supporters gathered on the day could barely say anything other than 'Yessss'.

While none of them could claim to have waited the whole 114 years, Swindon Town Football Club had toiled that long to reach the uppermost reaches of English football. But more recently there had been a burning desire to see the perceived unfairness administered by football's authorities in 1990 overturned, and for Town to claim what they saw as their just desserts. Mission accomplished.

But the expected celebratory bus tour took place amid rumour that something was in the air.

Hoddle met the board on 2 June, with the understanding that Chelsea wanted Town's newest hero to become their manager. The following day the *Advertiser*'s headline was '48 hours to keep Hoddle'.

The continued cash shortage that the manager had experienced during his time at the County Ground seemed to have at last taken its toll, an issue which Ken Bates at Stamford Bridge was likely to have less problem with, while convincing his target to join his club.

There was very little that chairman Ray Hardman could ever have done to convince the ambitious Hoddle to have remained in Wiltshire. The logical, head-led decision of taking the reins of cash-flush Chelsea, well established in the top flight, would have trumped anything that heart-led emotion of staying with a newly promoted club, always one step from poverty, could have offered.

Before the triumphant day at Wembley, Hardman had commented, 'The financial reward for reaching the Premier League is enormous. It probably adds up to at least £1m.' Thirty years later, that prize for promotion to the Premier League was accepted to be 180 times higher.

Swindon Town had never had more to offer, and it still wasn't enough to convince Hoddle to stay; the raw elation of promotion to the Premier League was doused by the departure of the man who had made it happen.

Much has been made of Hoddle's use of a diamond midfield at the County Ground. The formation was built around the solid defensive partnership of Colin Calderwood and Shaun Taylor; a chalk and cheese duo whose strengths complemented each other so successfully.

When that pairing was augmented with the presence of Hoddle, sometimes operating as a traditional sweeper, sometimes stepping in front of the two to allow greater range to his passing excellence, the whole shape of the team was defined.

The midfield was allowed greater opportunity to influence attacks; the wing-backs afforded the space and freedom to maraud down the flanks.

Hoddle anchored the base of the diamond and deployed his own immense talents, or was effectively deputised by the born-again Ross MacLaren, who was demonstrating that there was far more to his game than had originally been believed before the arrival of Ossie Ardiles unveiled his full potential.

It was a method which showcased the skills of Town's players and was undeniably enhanced by Hoddle, but in truth, much of the style under him had begun to see the light of day at the County Ground during Ardiles's time.

Under Ossie, Alan McLoughlin had become a revelation when played behind the front two, a huge change in the direction of the career of the ex-Manchester United man as the midfield diamond was introduced to the watching public. But despite the loss of McLoughlin, it needed the arrival of Hoddle to complete the fourth corner.

Hoddle polished the system, added his own undoubted ability to the side and and trusted the rest of the players to use their developing skills. But the foundation laid by Ardiles prior to Hoddle's arrival could not be overstated.

After the celebration and elation of gaining promotion to the Premier League had subsided, there was a satisfying sense of conclusion-ism. That a wrong had been righted. This time the prize was Town's to keep.

The season had begun with victory over Sunderland, who had been promoted to the top flight in place of Swindon in 1990. That result came through Hoddle's 55th-minute strike, the first of the season and the first of his Swindon career.

Then the season finished with Hoddle's last goal in a Town shirt, the opening strike of a match at Wembley which brought promotion to the burgeoning Premier League.

Those two goals bookended a campaign that culminated 114 years of Swindon Town history by elevating the club to the elite for the first time.

In 1993, the rewards of the Premier League were not what they would become, but these were the days when victory seemed as much about glory as financial gain. And Swindon's Wembley triumph was glorious.

As a supporter I remember departing Wembley in 1990 after watching my team annihilate the opposition and seeing distraught Sunderland fans sitting, head in hands, on the steps of a pub. Identifying in the desolation one was clearly feeling, I called out of the car window for him to keep believing. Next year might be different.

His weary, silent response was one of resignation and spoke volumes, and I have often pondered how this plainly dedicated Mackem felt when ten days later he heard the news that his team were promoted after all, and Swindon weren't. Did he think of me, I wonder.

Football supporters are all as helpless as each other.

Wembley 1990. Sunderland goalkeeper Tony Norman is helplessly grounded as Alan McLoughlin's deflected shot gives Town the lead.

Wembley 1990. Steve White's shot hits the post and Duncan Shearer is about to make an inelegant attempt to turn in the rebound.

Wembley 1990. The scoreboard fails to convey the magnitude of an overwhelming Swindon Town victory.

Wembley 1990. Skipper Colin Calderwood hoists the trophy which should confirm top-flight football for Swindon Town.

Manager Ossie and goalscorer Alan Mac celebrate Wembley victory in 1990.

Glenn Hoddle and John Gorman sign on as manager and assistant manager of Swindon Town on 4 April 1991.

Duncan Shearer scores his fourth of the match at Plymouth Argyle in October 1991.

Dave Mitchell forces a save in the 1-1 draw at Portsmouth in March 1992.

Steve White scores Town's third goal of the day on his way to a hat-trick against Watford in March 1993.

Penalty king Paul Bodin beats Pavel Srnicek to equalise in the 2-1 win over runaway Division One champions Newcastle in March 1993.

Glenn Hoddle showing unusual aerial endeavour in the nine-man, goalless draw at Brentford in March 1993.

Dave Mitchell completes the scoring in the 90th minute to bring the scoreline to a breathless Birmingham 4 Swindon Town 6 in April 1993.

Dave Mitchell nets the second of the match in the third minute in the Division One play-off semi-final against Tranmere Rovers at the County Ground on 16 May 1993.

Dave Mitchell and Colin Calderwood are happy having reached the Division One play-off final with aggregate victory at Tranmere on 19 May 1993.

Colin Calderwood tussles with Marco Gabbiadini. Wembley 1993.

Craig Maskell has just put Swindon Town 2-0 up. Wembley 1993.

Wembley 1993. Shaun Taylor dives in with classic bravery to score Swindon Town's third goal of the Division Two play-off final.

Wembley 1993. Paul Bodin scores the 84th-minute penalty to seal promotion to the Premier League for Swindon Town.

Wembley 1993. The four goalscorers. Paul Bodin, Craig Maskell, Glenn Hoddle and Shaun Taylor show off the trophy their goals have won.

Wembley 1993. Shaun Taylor, Dave Mitchell and Martin Ling celebrate Swindon Town's victory over Leicester City to claim promotion to the Premier League.

John Moncur shows his determination at White Hart Lane in the 1-1 draw with Tottenham Hotspur in October 1993.

[Above, left]: Fraser Digby and Liverpool's Ian Rush compete for the ball in the 2-2 draw at Anfield in December 1993. [Above right]: Shaun Taylor powers above Aston Villa's Andy Townsend. Martin Ling and John Moncur look on. February 1994. [Right]: January 1994. Jan-Åge Fjørtoft tussles with Colin Calderwood on his way to his first Premier League goal, as Swindon claim the third win of the campaign in a 2-1 victory over Tottenham Hotspur.

5
1993/94

WHEN EVERYONE returned for pre-season training, so much was new.

There was a new manager, new record signings, an apparently spurious moving of midweek home fixtures from Tuesday nights to Wednesdays, squad numbers were introduced to replace the old 1–11 positional identifiers, three substitutes could be named, and there was a new Premier League status for Swindon Town.

As Glenn Hoddle had left the County Ground on 3 June with Chelsea his destination, he believed his long-term friend and deputy John Gorman was right behind him. Both had agreed to join Ken Bates's Stamford Bridge outfit and were scheduled to travel directly from Swindon to meet Bates before signing their new contracts.

What Hoddle didn't know as he drove away was that Gorman was being intercepted by Swindon chairman Ray Hardman with an urgent request, 'I want you to stay and be our new manager.'

It presented Gorman with a dilemma. The opportunity to manage in the Premier League was something that all coaches would aspire to. As Hoddle controlled things on the pitch, John had been accustomed to being entrusted with matchday activities from the touchline. As such he could surely lay claim to much of the credit for promotion.

It could only be expected that anyone in that position would be curious to test his abilities with ultimate authority. Professional ambition would unquestionably dictate that any second-in-command would want to try out his own top-level managerial credentials.

Gorman asked for time to consider Hardman's approach but found that his decision was made far more quickly than he anticipated.

That evening he first spoke to Myra, his wife of 23 years, to tell her that he was staying at Swindon. She did not appear best pleased. He also spoke to Hardman to advise his chairman of his decision to accept the offer to become Town's new boss.

But the most difficult discussion of the three was when Gorman phoned his friend of approaching 20 years to tell Hoddle that he would be joining Chelsea on his own. Hoddle wasn't best pleased either.

The two men had first met at Tottenham Hotspur's training ground at Cheshunt in 1976 and had become firm friends. Once Hoddle had accepted Swindon's offer back in 1991, he had no hesitation in deciding who he wanted to accompany him as his deputy. Over the years the two would become almost inseparable as a managerial duo.

But this was to be the exception to the rule regarding their partnership.

Scotsman Gorman's playing career had started at Celtic, leaving for Carlisle United with just one cup appearance to his name. After 230 appearances at Brunton Park, including a season in the old First Division, Spurs manager Keith

Burkinshaw came calling with a £60,000 cheque to take Gorman to White Hart Lane.

Another 30 outings followed before a challenge from Jimmy Case in a match against Liverpool wrecked the ligaments and cartilage in Gorman's left knee and robbed him of the rest of his top-level playing career.

Encouraged to call an end to his playing days by Burkinshaw, Gorman had subsequently wondered whether that was a decision forced upon him too early, at the age of 29. Four seasons playing and coaching in the USA proved that his knee problems had not necessarily warranted such hasty action.

As a condition of releasing John from his contract, Spurs had insisted on a clause which prevented him from returning to play in England, but he, Myra and his family enjoyed the American experience so much that it didn't appear to be too much of a hardship.

An eventual move back home to the UK came in 1986 when he joined Gillingham, officially as chief scout, but where he also adopted the responsibilities of youth team and reserve team manager, and then first team assistant manager as he gained his full FA coaching badges. One of his early duties as part of the Gills' backroom team was to watch as Swindon triumphed over his new colleagues in the Third Division play-off final of 1986/87.

Despite being advised to call an end to his playing days years earlier, Gorman was still turning out for the Gills' reserve side past his 40th birthday, and a spell coaching at Leyton Orient followed.

When 33-year-old Hoddle made the call to invite Gorman, eight years his senior, to join him at Swindon it was certainly a greater professional challenge. Two years later, Ray Hardman's approach for him to take the helm offered him his first stab at managing a club. And that, at the pinnacle of the English game.

Gorman was now the new manager of Swindon, his iconic friend Hoddle was gone and both the Scot and the club faced the Premier League unknown together, but alone.

David Hay, an ex-Celtic team-mate, was appointed to the assistant manager's seat and the summer commenced with the usual round of contract discussions.

Eight players were offered new terms, while the rest were still under contract. Swindon had never before been able to dangle the carrot of top-flight football as an incentive to sign for the club, but still there was to be disappointment for Town fans.

Australian international Dave Mitchell, scorer of 15 goals during the promotion season, exercised an escape clause in his contract and departed for a short, ill-fated spell at Turkish club Altay S.K. for a mere £20,000.

And hugely respected centre-back and skipper Colin Calderwood rejected the chance to complete his journey from the Fourth Division to the Premier League while wearing a Town shirt. His decision to quit Wiltshire for Tottenham Hotspur, now managed by his old Swindon boss Ossie Ardiles, left a gaping hole in the centre of defence. Calderwood was plainly excited to join Tottenham on a four-year deal but said, 'It tugged the heartstrings to leave Swindon, but I had to take the chance at the age of 28.'

No one begrudged the loyal defender his move, which would lead to Scottish international caps, but similarly no one thought that the transaction would leave Town's defence anything other than weaker.

The deal would eventually cost Spurs £1.25m for a player who Town had acquired for £27,500 back in July 1985, but half of the fee was due to Mansfield Town, who had been granted an extremely lucrative sell-on clause by the transfer tribunal eight years previously.

That meant that almost the entire incoming sum was swallowed up by the £500,000 purchase of the well-regarded Adrian Whitbread from Leyton Orient as Calderwood's replacement. Also incoming was Dutch midfielder Luc Nijholt from Motherwell who cost £175,000, but with strikers being what strikers are, the most eye-catching Town signing of the summer was that of Norwegian international Jan-Åge Fjørtoft, who joined for another £500,000 from Rapid Vienna.

All three looked decent, and expensive, acquisitions. They were all to face the biggest test of their abilities.

With new sponsorship, the top flight had been branded the FA Carling Premiership and the marketing executives nominated a 'man to watch' from each of the 22 clubs.

Swindon's was to be Martin Ling, man of the match at Wembley in May. Tottenham's, meanwhile, was Stephen Carr. With no disrespect to either man, it didn't go unnoticed that collectively they were CarrLing, but reports that an unnamed, publicity-hungry club were preparing a bid for fictitious African striker Fizi Lah'Ga remained unsubstantiated.

Before August was out, the County Ground was scheduled to host Liverpool. In September it would be Manchester City, and before the end of the month would come a trip to Old Trafford to face their Manchester neighbours. Tottenham in October, Leeds United in November, Arsenal in December. This was going to be tough, but who thought it would be anything different?

Saturday, 14 August brought Swindon Town's Premier League debut, an away fixture at Bramall Lane to face Sheffield United. The Blades were no slouches, but not necessarily the first name to come to mind when considering the behemoths of the Premier League. Relegation had been avoided by just three points the previous season.

With Oldham Athletic due to visit the County Ground the following Wednesday, was this an early opportunity for Swindon to get their first points on the board within the first week?

Town's sheet remained clean in the Steel City for just 21 minutes. Nijholt was first dispossessed, then fouled the man who had the temerity to do it. The resultant free kick was headed on, where Willie Falconer became the first man to breach Swindon's defence in the Premier League.

The match was being played at a frantic pace under scorching conditions, and the Robins were quickly learning two lessons: how difficult it was to create chances, and how difficult it was to prevent the opposition from doing so.

But, still behind as the second half began, Craig Maskell was fouled 25 yards from goal. John Moncur then took advantage of indecisive organisation in the Blades' defence to place an early, exquisitely accurate low ball past goalkeeper Alan Kelly to equalise. Swindon had their first Premier League goal.

Town went on to make a good showing of their Premier League credentials as both sides demonstrated their intentions for the coming season. Twenty minutes from the end, Fjørtoft was forced from the field with an ankle injury. Maskell then made a hash of a good opportunity from inside six yards before Sheffield United won another free kick 13 minutes from time. Another cross, another header, another Blades goal.

With no option other than to push for a second equaliser, six minutes from the end Swindon's defence was exposed to concede United's third of the afternoon.

A harsh lesson had been dispensed. Premier League football was brutally unforgiving.

'I thought we were well matched, but they got the breaks and had two good set pieces,' said Gorman afterwards, in what was his first matchday in charge of a team. 'You can't give away silly free kicks on the edge of the box.'

On Wednesday, 18 August chairman Ray Hardman introduced supporters to Swindon's first home top-flight match in his programme notes, 'For the first time since the club's formation well over a century ago, the County Ground hosts a game at the very pinnacle of English professional football.' He concluded, 'Let us hope in May I am able to write to you in the programme having consolidated our position in the FA Premier League. I'm sure the team will not let you down.'

Oldham had avoided relegation on goal difference the previous season. Logic might have suggested they could have been the weakest team Town would face all season, and this with home advantage.

The Latics travelled to stifle Town's game by swamping the midfield with five men, effectively stopping the supply of crosses and passes to front men Maskell and Fjørtoft. The result was a stalemate in which, while chances were sporadically created by both sides, poor finishing looked likely to lead to both gaining their first point of the season.

Until the 90th minute. With new Town captain Ross MacLaren trying to regain and refit an errant boot, Norwegian international Gunnar Halle crossed to Paul Bernard to head home and claim all three points for the visitors.

Gorman's assessment was, 'It was bad enough losing the game at Sheffield in the last 15 minutes, but to lose a game like that was a real killer. It just goes to show that the Premiership demands total concentration for 90 minutes plus.'

Of the four goals conceded so far, three had been headers, while the game against Oldham had been notable for Swindon's inability to find a pass through a crowded midfield.

After just two matches it would have been foolish to have made any meaningful observations, but a few months earlier Colin Calderwood had won countless defensive headers, while as a deep-lying playmaker Glenn Hoddle had dictated play from outside the midfield congestion. And neither were still with the club.

Next up were Liverpool, by which time Gorman had moved to secure the signature of striker Andy Mutch from Wolverhampton Wanderers in a £250,000 deal. That dismantled his prolific partnership with Steve Bull, and the boyhood Liverpool supporter was to step straight into the team for the County Ground encounter alongside Fjørtoft.

The TV cameras came to Swindon on Sunday, 22 August, and what they showed the country was an unmistakeable demonstration of the gulf in class between the two sides.

MacLaren moved to the deep sweeper role recently vacated by Hoddle as Town resurrected a formation similar to that which had proved so successful the previous season.

Nijholt moved to the front of a defensive diamond and Mutch replaced 1992/93 top scorer Maskell up front.

John Moncur produced a magnificent early crossfield pass to Mutch, who cantered clear of the offside trap to place his shot wide of Bruce Grobbelaar's goal with the game scoreless, but just short of 20 minutes in, Liverpool took the lead through Neil Ruddock.

Then Steve McManaman added a second from a fast-raiding break before half-time. Moncur and Martin Ling both had chances to reduce the deficit, but Fjørtoft missed the best opportunity to open his account, heading straight into the arms of Grobbelaar from a Kevin Horlock cross.

Even then, Fjørtoft and Mutch both had chances, but McManaman showed them how it was done with his second of the match on 61 minutes. A Ronnie Whelan 20-yarder and a Mike Marsh effort ten minutes from time completed the 5-0 rout.

Three games in, nine goals conceded and on that evening's *Sports Report* Liverpool sat top with nine points from nine, while Swindon sat bottom with none.

An optimist would have noticed that the only other team in the Premier League without a point were Southampton, and that was the destination for the Robins the following midweek. Wouldn't a sharing of the points be acceptable to both teams?

It seemed not. Two goals from Matt Le Tissier, and singles from Jeff Kenna, Iain Dowie and Neil Maddison silenced the moans from the home fans who had been calling for the head of manager Ian Branfoot. A late penalty from Maskell, on as a substitute for Fjørtoft, did little to lend proceedings an air of respectability as Town conceded five for the second time in four days.

'We were written off before the season started and people will be writing us off after this result,' Gorman told the *Advertiser*, 'but we will continue to play our football and do our best to prove them wrong.' Gorman made the point that time to work on the training pitch between matches was scarce. There had been just one day's training between the massacre by Liverpool, switched to Sunday at the demand of TV execs, and the trip to the south coast for another mauling.

In truth Town were creating chances, but with confidence in front of goal decimated, they were going to waste. Fjørtoft had still to get off the mark while Mutch hadn't hit the ground running as was needed.

If it had been known then that Mutch would need another four appearances before finding the net, and that Fjørtoft would need almost another five months, it would have been too much for Town fans to bear.

Neither man scored at Norwich City in the last game of August, but the fact that the Canaries didn't either sweetened the pill a little. A 0-0 draw away from home at last gave Town their first Premier League point, and their first clean sheet of the season.

September opened with a Wednesday evening visit of Manchester City, and just as at Carrow Road four days earlier Gorman opted for a 4-5-1 formation with a flat back four, a packed midfield and Andy Mutch alone up front. The boss was desperately trying to determine the best setup for his troops.

City were in disarray after the sacking of manager Peter Reid, with the players rumoured to be ready to revolt at the decision, and chances were plentiful for both sides. Nicky Summerbee in particular revelled in a wide-right midfield role and Micky Hazard was at his influential best.

As a result of Moncur seeing his penalty saved by Tony Coton after Summerbee had been felled in the box, the game remained scoreless for an hour. Adrian Whitbread's 30-yard effort had been easily dealt with by Coton, Hazard's snap shot just missed the target and Ling netted, only for the ball to be called back for a Town free kick.

The set piece was taken by Summerbee, whose shot took a deflection which fooled Coton and Swindon had their first goal in front of their own home fans since 16 May. There was half an hour to play.

Unfortunately, it had already been proved that it would be more than enough time for points to slip through Town's fingers. In the last 15 minutes Michel Vonk grabbed a scrambled equaliser, Niall Quinn added to it and substitute Adie Mike increased the margin in the last minute.

It was possibly the best performance that Swindon had produced so far, and it still wasn't enough to avoid a 3-1 defeat.

The defensive numbers had been reinforced by the arrival of former England international Terry Fenwick from Tottenham on 6 September, and that was soon to be augmented by the return to fitness of Paul Bodin, who had been injured in pre-season and had been absent so far. The division's leakiest defence needed all the assistance it could muster.

Upton Park was the next venue for the Swindon Town roadshow as the Robins travelled to London to face West Ham United, who were too close to the bottom of the table for manager Billy Bonds to feel comfortable. One point off the drop zone, it could be used as a motivational tool that Swindon could go level on points with the Hammers were they to win.

Town did their best, in particular Fraser Digby. Ever present so far, Digby produced an inspired display to ensure that the Robins left with their goals against column further unsullied in a second successive goalless outcome away from home.

Fjørtoft started up front with Mutch, but as was becoming regular, the Norwegian was hooked from the field with 20 minutes to play. Patience was beginning to wear thin as the big-fee striker was yet to come good.

Again Hazard, Summerbee and Moncur shone in midfield, but a mistake from Nijholt left Digby exposed, forcing him to head the ball clear under pressure from Trevor Morley. Digby then had to deal with powerful efforts from Julian Dicks and Matthew Holmes and reserved his best stop from Steve Jones with just four minutes remaining.

Post-match, Gorman assessed his strikers, 'I had enough faith in their ability to sign them and that has not changed despite our lack of goals. They are nervous because they want to score and being anxious, they are snatching at chances.' On the performance more generally he said, 'The quality of our play was there for all to see. We certainly didn't play like a team at the bottom of the table.' Gorman also called Digby's performance 'outstanding'.

Digby was also happy, 'I've never lost faith in my own ability. I've played around 300 times for Swindon, and I'm experienced enough to know I have to take the rough with the smooth.'

The style in which Town were playing was bringing some appreciative comments from observers. Liverpool boss Graeme Souness had said after his team had visited the County Ground, 'You have to admire Swindon for the way they play their football. It could have been so different if they had scored with one of their early opportunities. They may start to believe they shouldn't be in this league, but that's definitely not the case.'

Very welcome comments from such a luminary figure. But when Souness finished with, 'Lady Luck was with us and we went on to win the game,' there was a sense of condescension about the well-meant words from a manager who had just seen his side win 5-0.

Back at home in mid-September, Kevin Keegan's Newcastle United came to town, with summer signing Peter Beardsley available after injury. Gorman was pleased that at last he had a full squad to choose from, with Bodin back to match fitness and Fenwick available for his first Town match.

Both teams had claimed promotion the previous season and with the Magpies seven points ahead of Swindon in the table, the First Division champions had certainly made the better start.

And post-match, Keegan was also vocal in his assessment of Swindon, 'I've heard it said that Swindon don't deserve to be in the Premier League – well don't you believe it. They are a super footballing side. I watched them against Liverpool and for 20 minutes they had one of the best sides in the country on the rack!'

With less than ten minutes to half-time the score was still 0-0, and much of the action had been at the Newcastle end of the pitch. Mutch failed to get a shot away by delaying too long, Fjørtoft's volley just missed the target and Bodin fired over the bar from less than ten yards.

Even when Lee Clark scored at the near post, Bodin was presented with the immediate chance to equalise from the spot after a foul on Moncur. But Town's regular penalty taker uncharacteristically fired the ball at the legs of the diving Tommy Wright to spurn the opportunity.

There was still time for referee Howard King to point to the other 12-yard spot where Malcolm Allen made no mistake in doubling the visitors' lead before the half-time whistle blew. Two goals down was scarcely what Swindon deserved.

Summerbee and Fjørtoft both came close to hitting the target in the second half, before on the hour Nijholt spotted Fjørtoft, whose clever dummy left Ling one-on-one with Wright. He drew the keeper and coolly finished the move to get his team back in it.

Two minutes later, and with the volume of noise from the 15,000 crowd building, Ling and Bodin combined excellently down the Town left. Bodin's cross was met by the arriving Mutch, who celebrated his first Swindon goal with a cartwheel as he levelled.

Another point for Town but after eight games the Robins still sought their first win. The three draws meant that if that win was to come the following week, Swindon could lift themselves level on points with fourth-bottom Sheffield Wednesday.

The problem was that 25 September brought a trip to Old Trafford.

Unsurprisingly, Swindon ran out against reigning Premier League champions Manchester United in front of the biggest crowd they had seen since their Wembley play-off victory. Over 44,000 were in attendance, and while every head expected to see Town comprehensively beaten, several thousand travelling Wiltshire hearts hoped differently.

Five minutes in, Andrei Kanchelskis applied convention, placing Eric Cantona's pass into Fraser Digby's net to start the scoring. But soon home goalkeeper Peter Schmeichel was called into action to foil Hazard, Mutch and Ling, whose goal-bound efforts showed that Swindon were not prepared to be overawed.

Lee Sharpe thumped the ball against the woodwork before Fjørtoft blazed a shot over the bar at the other end. Summerbee watched as his 25-yard shot was turned over by Schmeichel, then Cantona finished a Sharpe pass to extend United's lead to 2-0 four minutes before the break.

Digby countered further efforts from Sharp and Kanchelskis and Ince hammered the ball against the crossbar. Everyone in attendance, regardless of their allegiance, was getting their money's worth. Six minutes into the second period, Hazard lost possession, Sharpe's cross found the head of Mark Hughes and it was 3-0.

If everything was going the way of those led by their heads, the hearts were about to get a look in.

Twelve minutes from the end, Mutch got his head to a Hazard cross and the ex-Wolves man had his second goal in two matches. And when substitute Steve White, on for Fjørtoft, was clattered by Gary Pallister in the 85th minute, the shout for a penalty from the Swindon supporters was ignored by referee Joe Worral to much consternation.

But only for three minutes. Then it was Steve Bruce who made his own clumsy challenge on White, Worral pointed to the spot and Bodin struck it high past Schmeichel; 3-2 with the final whistle imminent.

Town, with nothing to lose but glory to gain, committed everything to the third goal, only for Hughes to grab his second and United's fourth in the last minute.

White was most upset afterwards. 'It was a penalty. No question about it,' he said regarding Worral's refusal to penalise the first challenge. 'I chased down a pass and Pallister definitely brought me down. I'm not going to go down for nothing in that sort of position. We came so close to getting back on level terms. At one stage it was only their goalkeeper keeping them in it.'

Once more the statistics showed that Swindon had been beaten, and this time after conceding four against the Premier League champions. No one outside the town would care, or believe, that but for a non-decision by the referee with five minutes to go, they might have fought back for an incredible 3-3 draw.

And at the end of the campaign it would only be the statistics that counted.

By this stage of the season there was nothing new about the Premier League experience. There was a weary realisation that Swindon needed more than they'd been able to offer so far to compete. They were giving it their best shot every time they took to the pitch, but it was being proved to be not enough.

It wasn't quite acceptance, but it was an understanding that the step up from the First Division to the Premier League was even bigger than first believed. The euphoria of triumph at Wembley to fulfil a 114-year dream had dissipated rapidly. Swindon had played nine matches, almost a quarter of the season, and had faced almost half of the teams in the top flight. And the return was three points.

When October broke, Kenny Dalglish brought Blackburn Rovers to the County Ground. Duncan Shearer had been replaced by Alan Shearer after Jack Walker financed a £3.6m deal, helping Rovers finish second behind Manchester United the previous season. In contrast, £1m of Swindon talent was absent from the pitch. Adrian Whitbread was injured and Jan-Åge Fjørtoft was consigned to the bench as Steve White, a free transfer way back in 1986, made his second start of the season – his final start in a Swindon shirt.

Fraser Digby was again Town's best performer but nothing he could do could stop Shearer scoring twice, the first after 15 minutes and the latter a minute from time. In between, old warhorse Shaun Taylor netted a 32nd-minute equaliser with a classic powerful header, but Stuart Ripley's 51st-minute strike restored the visitors' lead.

John Gorman lost his temper after the 3-1 defeat, describing the performance as the worst yet.

Taylor was on the scoresheet for the second Premier League match running in a 1-1 home draw with Everton in the middle of October, then Bodin got in on the act with penalties at Tottenham and at home to Aston Villa.

The match at White Hart Lane produced another 1-1 draw and the general consensus was that Swindon thoroughly deserved at least the one point they left with. It was attended by over 31,000 people, the biggest gate at the home of Tottenham so far that season, with the kick-off delayed by ten minutes to allow the crowd to take their seats, such was the attraction for the Londoners to see the might of John Gorman's men take on those led by Ossie Ardiles and featuring ex-Swindon captain Colin Calderwood.

It brought a homecoming for John Moncur and Terry Fenwick, and each were to endeavour to show their past employers what they had lost. Ross MacLaren and Jan-Åge Fjørtoft also had their best games so far and four minutes in, Andy Mutch forced a quick block from goalkeeper Erik Thorstvedt.

The travelling supporters might have been rubbing their eyes when Fjørtoft let fly with a stunning shot from the edge of the penalty box which his international colleague did well to hold, then Moncur collected a Fjørtoft flick and tried a 30-yard chip which the busy keeper just reached with his fingertips.

Goalless at half-time, the home side had looked distinctly second best, but Town supporters had seen this script too many times before and six minutes into the second half Jason Dozzell bypassed two defenders to neatly finish past Digby.

Mutch was almost immediately felled in the box to no reaction from Keren Barrett, but when Taylor suffered the same fate, the referee pointed to the spot. Bodin did what Bodin did best, hammering home the spot kick, and the stage was set for a Swindon winner, which Fjørtoft, Moncur and substitute Horlock all failed in their efforts to achieve.

The game was yet another in which Town had failed to collect the points their performance appeared to deserve, but endeavour and stylish intention were becoming little consolation for being rooted to the bottom of the table.

When Aston Villa came to the County Ground on Halloween and Bodin scored his customary penalty, it gave Swindon a 33rd-minute lead which yet again they failed to protect. Already back on level terms by half-time, another Villa goal midway through the second half meant that the previous season's runners-up took all three points back to the Midlands with a 2-1 victory.

Not only was everything becoming so predictable for Town fans, but there was also an increasing feeling that time and fixtures were slipping away quickly. Despondent supporters were beginning to make their disappointment heard. The table showed a massive 29-point gap between leaders Manchester United and the Robins at the bottom, but far more meaningfully, they were already six points from relegation safety.

As November began it was announced that midfielder Micky Hazard was in the throes of completing a cut-price £50,000 return to Tottenham to link up again with Ardiles, while ex-Town loanee Roy Wegerle was being considered for a move back to the County Ground from Coventry City.

Hazard moved, Wegerle didn't, and Town moved on to a 3-0 defeat at Wimbledon. The season had been running for three months, just five points had been claimed and incredibly the Robins were still looking for their first win.

An international break meant Town took a rest from the relentless pressure of Premier League competition ahead of the visit of Ipswich Town on 20 November. When the Blues arrived in Wiltshire, Swindon's bank account was £300,000 lighter and Gorman had a new striker.

The sum had been invested to prise Keith Scott from Wycombe Wanderers; Fjørtoft had been relieved of his first-team shirt. Ipswich sat 14th in the table and under pressure Gorman had spoken to the *Evening Advertiser* pleading for more patience, 'We are bottom, and we have to get off it. Two wins will do it and our next two games against Ipswich and QPR at home are the most important.'

Ray Hardman was sympathetic towards his manager, 'It's no good shouting for John Gorman's head. That would do nothing at all. What this club needs is 150 per cent support.'

Such numerical impossibilities were hopefully not representative of overly optimistic financial budgetary in the boardroom.

Town had the boost of a new striker, and also the return of Paul Bodin, who had experienced the disappointment of missing a penalty for Wales which could have taken his country to the World Cup finals in the USA. How heavily would that weigh on the defender's mind?

As it happened, both men played key roles in claiming a sixth point of the campaign, and once again the Robins attempted to demonstrate their worthiness to be in exalted top-flight company.

The visitors took a 17th-minute lead through John Wark, making his 600th appearance for the Suffolk club, and by then Mutch had already seen a goal disallowed for offside. A goal behind, Ling had hit the woodwork, Scott, Taylor and Horlock all tested goalkeeper Clive Baker, and Moncur saw his 25-yarder touched over the bar.

At last, just before the break, Terry Fenwick crossed for Scott to mark his debut with a thumping header for his 15th goal of the season – his first for his new employers.

Wark was again on the mark for Ipswich 20 minutes into the second half, but Bodin claimed the ball after a clumsy challenge by Eddie Youds, this time to successfully convert his second spot kick of the week to make the score 2-2.

Scott's assessment of his first top-level match was, 'The pace was extraordinary – a lot quicker than I expected.'

Fifteen games in, six points won, six points from safety, already 35 goals conceded. Games won; none. The media were making comparisons with Swindon's form and the worst start to a top-flight season, suffered by Sheffield United in 1990/91 when the Blades went 16 games without a win.

Wednesday, 24 November brought the visit of Queens Park Rangers to the County Ground, a team just two points behind second-placed Aston Villa. It would be Swindon's 16th game of the season. History beckoned.

Eighteen minutes in, Luc Nijholt was unhappy about being penalised for a challenge and spoke his mind to referee Gerald Ashby; the initial yellow card was upgraded to red.

What odds would have been given on ten-man Swindon making history and claiming their first Premier League victory, especially when Fraser Digby watched as a Rangers header cannoned off his crossbar?

But with eight minutes of the first half remaining, Bodin crossed into the QPR box, Mutch knocked the ball towards his new strike partner, and Scott stabbed it home from close range. Scott had been a Swindon player for six days, and over the course of four of them he had scored twice.

What followed was 50 minutes of backs-to-the-wall endeavour from Gorman's ten men. Fenwick, Horlock, Whitbread, Digby and Taylor performed heroics, flinging themselves at everything that the Hoops could throw at them, and when the final whistle blew Swindon had got their first win of the season at the 16th attempt. The pitch invasion that followed was a demonstration of a huge outpouring of relief.

Frustratingly, an unlikely victory for Southampton at Aston Villa meant that Town's gap to relegation safety had been reduced by just one point, from six to five, but the evening was to be one of hope rather than continued despondency.

Three days later, the newly emboldened Robins travelled to Elland Road to take on Leeds United, and with ten minutes to go the score stood at 0-0. Then Leeds legend Gordon Strachan set about creating three goals as he single-handedly gave the scoreline a magnitude it barely warranted. The 3-0 result lifted the home side to second in the table and brought yet another brutal crash course in Premier League reality for Swindon.

As December dawned it brought a horrifying glimpse of potential déjà vu. The first four games of the month brought the reverse fixtures of the first four matches of the season. In August, Swindon had lost to Sheffield United, Oldham Athletic, Liverpool and Southampton. Now they faced all four again. What had been learned in the ensuing three months?

Three out of the four results would bring an improvement, starting at home to Sheffield United when a goalless draw added a point to the total.

Next came a visit to Boundary Park. In August, Oldham had taken all three points with a 1-0 win at the County Ground. This time the points stayed in their possession, but by a 2-1 scoreline.

A trip to Anfield to face Liverpool, 5-0 winners in Wiltshire in the summer, would have brought the greatest trepidation for Gorman's team. This time though things were different.

'Brave. Brilliant. Breathtaking.' These were the first three words in the *Evening Advertiser*'s match report on Monday, 13 December. 'Bottom club Swindon's performance at Anfield on Saturday was all these and more,' added the paper.

After an hour the game was still waiting for its first goal. Then good passing interchanges involving the outstanding Moncur, Scott and Summerbee saw Summerbee make the Liverpool penalty box in front of the Kop. He evaded the attention of John Barnes and crossed perfectly for Moncur to slide home past Bruce Grobbelaar.

The Reds responded, and a header from Barnes just evaded Digby to square the score 11 minutes later. But just three minutes after that, Horlock's purposeful run created a chance for Mutch. His header was only blocked by Grobbelaar and Scott was on hand to finish the move. Liverpool were stunned, and forced Town into a rearguard action; the last in a succession of corners found Mark Wright, whose header made the score 2-2 four minutes from the final whistle.

After Swindon had been applauded off the field by the impressed and appreciative Merseysiders, Gorman commented, 'People keep having a knock at us, but we keep coming back. I think this proved once and for all that we should be in the Premier League.'

Graeme Souness added, 'Swindon came here to play football, and they did it very well.' Less praise than he had given Town earlier in the season, but in August he had just watched his team win 5-0. Was this proof that Swindon were making progress, and if so, just how taciturn might Souness have been if Swindon had held on to win?

The big boys could indulge their upstart younger sibling until such time as they became a threat.

A week before Christmas Day, Southampton, 5-1 winners at The Dell back in August, arrived at the County Ground to try their hand at a repeat performance. The Saints' season hadn't gone well since, with the south coast club just one place and three points ahead of the bottom-placed Robins.

After 12 minutes Bodin battled against a strong wind, beat two defenders and left Dave Beasant helpless with a strong left-footed shot. Matt Le Tissier equalised seven minutes from the break, but with the wind at their backs Town forced the pace.

Scott went close, Mutch's header went wide after a deflection, then on 65 minutes Swindon took the lead once more, and again man of the match Bodin was the architect. His corner found Scott on the far post and the 6ft 3in striker dived in to win it. The result left Town bottom, but level on points with the Saints on 14.

Both teams had scored 19 times but the Robins' horrendous goals against column meant there was a huge gap of ten in goal difference. This had been Town's best chance to get off the bottom of the Premier League.

Scott had scored four times in seven matches and with Fjørtoft an unused substitute, his goals were proving crucial. How unfortunate then that exactly halfway through the season, he'd already scored his last.

The four December matches had returned five points, while the corresponding games earlier in the season had yielded none. It seemed that Town may have been adjusting to the demands of the Premier League, but it would need a continued resurgence to offer any hope of avoiding the drop.

A 4-0 defeat at home to Arsenal a day after Boxing Day didn't fit the bill. If Santa had looked at John Gorman's list prior to Christmas, he'd have fallen down on the checking it twice duties. Kevin Campbell grabbed a hat-trick, Ian Wright grabbed the fourth with an audacious last-minute chip, and Swindon had succumbed to their biggest losing margin since August.

Throughout the season Gorman attempted to counter the lack of top-level nous in his squad by adding experience. Terry Fenwick, Brian Kilcline, Celtic striker Frank McAvennie and Wimbledon FA Cup scoring hero Lawrie Sanchez all came in with vast footballing backgrounds, but perhaps an increasing hope that experienced recruitment alone could make the difference was misplaced.

Gorman was to comment years later that by adding such players to his squad he was also bringing in opinion. Opinion which sometimes went to the detriment of his own instructions.

Intending to play a three-man defence against the Gunners, Gorman was convinced to revert to a flat back four by the view of the dressing room, and when his side took to the pitch he watched as they played an unsuccessful offside trap which also went contrary to the manager's game plan.

The implication was that it was one of these new players who had been responsible for the heavy defeat.

When Town travelled to Hillsborough to take on Sheffield Wednesday three days before 1994 commenced, it was a chance to see out the most momentous year in the club's history with one last hurrah.

With Scott destined not to find the net again all season and Fjørtoft a regular fixture on the bench, there was relief when Mutch scored his fourth of the campaign after seven minutes, only for Mark Bright to equalise a minute later. Then Craig Maskell (apparently despondent at results and opportunities, and on Town's transfer list) added his first goal since August and Swindon entered the dressing room at half-time with the advantage.

The turning point came in the 69th minute when home striker Gordon Watson collided with Fraser Digby, leaving the keeper on the floor. With everyone waiting for the referee's whistle, Phil Don waved play on, and Watson completed his task by knocking the ball into an unattended net.

Having dislocated a shoulder, Digby was replaced by Nicky Hammond for his first Premier League appearance, and Hammond's first task was to retrieve the ball from his net as Watson scored his second inside two minutes.

With the whistle-averse referee Don considering blowing for the end of the match, Ling's trickery found Mutch, whose cross was met by Maskell to finish the scoring with a brave diving header and secure a 3-3 draw.

The away point was welcome but growing increasingly insufficient. Digby would be out for almost two months, but it looked as though in Mutch a new solution to the striking problems may have been found from a previously undervalued source.

January brought a familiar face to the County Ground and a sadly familiar outcome. Glenn Hoddle arrived with his Chelsea side on New Year's Day and left with all three points courtesy of a 3-1 win, putting to an end a run of 22 away games without victory. The only bright spot for Swindon was a second goal in two matches from Mutch.

Two days later Mutch did it again, this time grabbing a 90th-minute equaliser at Highfield Road to claim a point with a televised 1-1 draw at Coventry City.

Three goals in three games for Mutch then, but just as with Keith Scott in December he had just scored his last of the season, this with four months still to run.

It was then announced that the much-heralded Norway international Jan-Åge Fjørtoft, mindful that he would not be selected for his country for the forthcoming World Cup without playing games, was rejoining Norwegian side Lillestrøm on loan in a bid to rediscover his scoring form. 'I'm disappointed that things haven't worked out for me at Swindon,' he said with an air of finality.

And to further compound the problem, Craig Maskell, the two-goal hero against Sheffield Wednesday at the end of December, had made his last start in a Town shirt and would be off to Southampton for £250,000 in little over a month, while Steve White was absent through a long-term injury.

When Town travelled to Goodison Park in the middle of January, they were nine points behind 15th-placed Everton and still four points from safety. Possibly the greatest indicator of all was their goal difference of -30. When they lost they tended to lose heavily, and this trip to Merseyside would be no different.

A goal down after five minutes, a second followed two minutes before the half-time whistle.

Four minutes into the second half Mutch, once on Everton's books at schoolboy level, elbowed John Ebbrell and referee Gerald Ashby – who had sent off Luc Nijholt in November – pulled out his red card once again.

Incredibly, ten-man Town fought back to level through Moncur and Bodin, but then an avalanche of Toffees goals brought a final score of 6-2. And still that wouldn't be the heaviest defeat of the season.

It never rains but it pours. What Town needed was a miracle, and when one arrived it came from the most unexpected source.

During the season Town had taken part in the usual cup competitions, but they had paled into insignificance in the shadow of the Premier League challenge. For the first time, when they took on Wolverhampton Wanderers in the League Cup, league placing superiority saw the Wiltshire side as the 'giants' rather than Wolves. Victory over the Black Country club was followed by elimination by Portsmouth in the next round, and few supporters could spare the enthusiasm to worry about it.

A 1-1 home draw with Ipswich Town in the FA Cup in January brought little interest, and neither would the 2-1 defeat in the replay at Portman Road. Except for one reason.

Record £500,000 signing Jan-Åge Fjørtoft, who had never quite finalised his loan spell back to Norway, scored his first goal six months after signing for the Robins.

Four days later, Tottenham Hotspur were due in Wiltshire. Ossie Ardiles and Colin Calderwood were back in town and Swindon were desperate for a response to the mammoth mauling suffered at Everton.

Mid-table Spurs were 14 points better off than Town, central defender Brian Kilcline had been signed from Newcastle and Mutch was still available ahead of a three-match suspension. Mutch and Fjørtoft started up front together for the first time since November.

Nick Barmby scored for the visitors after 30 minutes, but the goal came vastly against the run of play. Mutch had a header tipped over the bar, debutant Kilcline, who had replaced Fenwick in defence, threatened, and Ling hit the bar. Moncur had a chance from distance, and an injury to Erik Thorstvedt saw him replaced by Ian Walker, who soon needed to dive smartly to deal with a Taylor header.

As for Fjørtoft, he saw one shot go marginally wide, then he headed a long ball over Calderwood and followed up to equalise on 38 minutes. He had his first Premier League goal at last.

Things were less eventful in the second half, until ten minutes from the end when an indirect free kick inside the Tottenham penalty area brought the entire Spurs team back to the goal line. Nicky Summerbee struck a powerful shot from the set piece, it was blocked, and Adrian Whitbread grabbed his first goal for Town from the loose ball to seal a 2-1 win. Both £500,000 summer signings had made the scoresheet.

For once the Robins' superiority had brought the rewards it deserved, producing a victory against their illustrious London opponents as Fjørtoft scored his second goal in four days. At last Swindon's record investment was off the mark and everyone hoped Fjørtoft's form could finally match expectations.

Fjørtoft said of his earlier ordeal, 'I found the whole thing humiliating.' And of the mooted return to Norway, Gorman stated, 'He won't be going back.'

The following weekend brought another home fixture, this one against Coventry. A week had passed since Town had recorded what was only their third win of the season. Like Tottenham before them, Coventry were mid-table, well adrift from any title hopes or European qualification ambitions, and untroubled by any real relegation fears.

Nine minutes in a Summerbee corner reached the far post and Kilcline, whose powerful header proved too hot for Steve Ogrizovic in the Coventry goal to hold. Fjørtoft thrust his head into the ensuing melee and nodded the ball home to give Swindon the lead.

As the first half developed, Moncur was again outstanding in midfield while Kilcline set about a no-nonsense display at the back. Keith Scott just failed to reach a Moncur cross, and Ogrizovic was relieved to see a Kevin Horlock effort from 35 yards go narrowly wide.

Then in the 35th minute when Moncur was knocked unceremoniously to the ground in the Coventry penalty box, Fjørtoft undertook spot kick duties in the absence of the benched Bodin. Ogrizovic guessed right and got a hand to the Norwegian's strike, but its pace carried it into the net.

Coventry's Julian Darby rounded Nicky Hammond to pull a goal back in the 54th minute, but when Fjørtoft was manhandled to the deck he got up to send Ogrizovic the wrong way from 12 yards to grab his first hat-trick on English soil.

The 3-1 win meant Swindon had recorded consecutive victories for the first time, and Fjørtoft had scored five goals in three matches. Six points from two games and Town, while still bottom of the table, were just one win from hoisting themselves clear of the relegation zone. John Gorman said after the match, 'People are suddenly having to admit that we're not certainties to go down after all.'

Despite all that had gone before, with 14 games to go the Robins' tenacity had forced a tantalising glimpse of an escape route from what had seemed an impossible position. If Fjørtoft could keep scoring and the defence could tighten up, could it yet be possible to survive in the Premier League?

From a hard-won position of possibility, what followed over the next ten games was to define Swindon's season and ultimately their history.

A trip to Villa Park in mid-February proved disastrous. With Digby still out because of that dislocated shoulder and Hammond freshly added to the injury list, Jon Sheffield became the first of two loan goalkeepers to wear the shirt. He wouldn't have enjoyed the experience.

A hat-trick from Aston Villa's Dean Saunders and further strikes from Dalian Atkinson and Tony Daley left Town on the end of a 5-0 hiding. Then a 3-3 home draw with Norwich brought another brace of goals from Fjørtoft and an opener from Shaun Taylor but just one point.

And the pattern was set.

A 2-1 loss at Manchester City, a 1-1 draw at home to West Ham. A goal in each from Fjørtoft and one point from six. Over a two-month period, every time Town secured a point, the following match brought defeat.

The most damaging outcome came at Newcastle on 12 March. Fraser Digby was back in goal, and Moncur scored in the 78th minute. But by then the Magpies were already five goals to the good, and there was still time for two more for the home side before the final whistle.

The 7-1 defeat was the worst of a string of horrendous results throughout the season, and not the best preparation for the visit of Manchester United to the County Ground the following weekend.

The Red Devils, on their way to retaining their championship, took the lead through Roy Keane in the first half, then Luc Nijholt equalised with a tremendous 25-yard strike for his first goal for Swindon.

Paul Ince made it 2-1 to the visitors with just over an hour gone, then, four minutes later, United's headcount was reduced. Eric Cantona and Moncur tussled in midfield. Moncur, on his way to being crowned Swindon's Premier League Player of the Season, fell to the ground, and Cantona, apparently through sheer frustration, stamped on the prone midfielder's chest. Red card for Cantona, United down to ten men and over 20 minutes to play.

Swindon, counting recent signings Frank McAvennie and Lawrie Sanchez among their number, pressurised and with two minutes left, Peter Schmeichel's punch from a Taylor ball was returned by Whitbread. Scott and Sanchez failed to make meaningful contact, but Fjørtoft netted his tenth goal in nine games. Over 18,000 had witnessed events.

Following recently established convention, a Fjørtoft goal away at Blackburn Rovers in a 3-1 defeat was then followed by a draw. And one point from every six was plainly never going to retrieve the situation.

Having recently taken a point off Manchester United, a visit to Highbury to face Arsenal finished level when a Bodin penalty equalised Alan Smith's fifth-minute opener. Once again, a highly creditable performance and result – against the team third in the table – ended with Town drifting further from safety.

Seventh-placed Sheffield Wednesday's fixture in Wiltshire on 4 April was always destined for defeat for the home side, so substitute Gordon Watson's 69th-minute winner came as no surprise.

Three minutes earlier, Nicky Hammond had been helped from the pitch to be replaced by loan signing Paul Heald after Watson, the villain of the match at Hillsborough in December, had gashed Hammond's head with his studs. Whitbread was also stretchered off with damaged knee ligaments after a collision with Carlton Palmer, causing more selection issues for John Gorman.

The 1-0 defeat left Swindon 11 points from safety with just 15 to play for. Each passing match, every dropped point or three, had brought the finishing line and its inevitable doom into sharper focus.

On 14 April chairman Ray Hardman quantified the financial damage to Town's coffers should the inevitable happen and relegation ensue. The loss of around £1m in TV money alone would enforce player sales, but he pledged his support for Gorman.

Having just lost, when Fjørtoft scored after 14 minutes at Ipswich two weeks later, it was fore-written that Ian

Marshall's equaliser on the hour would seal a 1-1 draw. The drop loomed closer.

And it was finalised at the County Ground on 23 April, as the end of Swindon's Premier League adventure was finally confirmed. Nicky Summerbee's 67th-minute equaliser to John Fashanu's first-half goal was inconsequential against Wimbledon; the Dons scored four times in the last 20 minutes, and it helped Town's cause not one jot that one of them was an own goal.

At the end of the afternoon, Wimbledon had won 4-2 and Swindon were, as ever, at the foot of the Premier League table, on 27 points. There were three games to play, nine points to play for, and Town were 12 points from safety. The Football League was to be their destination once more.

A defeat at Chelsea was painful but not unexpected. The stuffing had been knocked out of Gorman's men for almost nine months. After his side's 2-0 win, Glenn Hoddle announced, 'I'm very sad to see Swindon go down. They have been to places like Liverpool, Arsenal and Tottenham and performed superbly without getting the rewards they deserved. I believe they have a very good chance of promotion [again].'

There were ten days of the season to go, and each of the remaining two matches would bring their own reason to be notable.

On the last day of April, Swindon undertook the journey to face QPR, who they had beaten in November for their first Premier League victory. Still seeking their first away win of the season, Town achieved it at the very last opportunity.

Halfway through the second period with the game still goalless, Shaun Taylor, who was soon to finish the season as an ever-present through the most testing of challenges, dived in among the boots to reach Moncur's free kick with his head to give Swindon the lead in his classic style. Having played every minute of the Premier League campaign, it was the leviathan defender's own inimitable bravery that epitomised the never-say-die, sometimes cavalier attitude of Gorman's team.

There had been multiple chances for both sides. Rangers hit Town's woodwork no fewer than three times and Les Ferdinand claimed an equaliser on 74 minutes. Town were denied a penalty and Fjørtoft watched as his looping header was clawed to safety. Bravely recalled and stitched up, Nicky Hammond made several important saves, and 13 minutes from time Keith Scott's cross allowed Fjørtoft to pounce and tuck away his 13th goal in 16 matches. Then with David Elleray's whistle poised, Bodin's pass to Summerbee in the QPR box was finished with aplomb to bring an almost surreal 3-1 win.

'Always look on the bright side of life' was heard from the travelling fans, and an ironic chant of 'easy, easy' demonstrated the gallows humour that only real football supporters can achieve.

After such comprehensive defeats throughout the season, Swindon's goals against column stood at 95 with one last match to play. Leeds were the visitors to the County Ground on 7 May, and there was a resigned atmosphere among the home supporters. Already confirmed as relegated, what further ignominy could possibly be heaped upon their club?

The figure of 100 goals conceded was close, and the Robins had already shipped five or more on five occasions. Surely it would be the height of cruelty for such indignity to round off their Premier League season.

In the 90th minute Chris Fairclough completed Gary Kelly's approach work to add to the previous four scored by the visiting team. Both sides had hit the woodwork, but only one had hit the net. Five times. Swindon had conceded 100 goals in their 42 matches.

It was particularly hard on loanee keeper Paul Heald, making his debut, but the previous ten months had proved just how unforgiving and brutal the Premier League was.

The season was one long litany of 'what ifs' and 'if onlys'. If only Hoddle and Calderwood hadn't departed before a ball had been kicked. If only Fjørtoft had started scoring earlier. If only the goals from Scott and Mutch hadn't dried up after promising spells.

What if Town had gained their first win earlier? If only they had gained the five points in August that they attained in December against the same four teams, would the early boost have turned hope into belief? Would the resultant confidence have been significant enough to inspire better results? Five points after the first four games would have seen Town lie 11th in the Prem table instead of being already adrift at the bottom.

But Swindon had been relegated by a 13-point margin.

Also taking the drop were Oldham Athletic and Sheffield United, the opposition for the opening two Premier League games. So, suspicions were proved correct. They were the weakest teams for Town to blood themselves against in August, and over the ten months they claimed just one of the 12 points available against them.

Not that there weren't also magnificent red-letter days in 1993/94. Town took points off champions Manchester United, third-placed Newcastle, fourth-placed Arsenal and a somewhat out of sorts eighth-placed Liverpool. But such days must be countered against the fact that Swindon conceded no fewer than 29 goals against the same opposition.

Over the course of the season Town's home gate averaged out at 14,021. Those with appropriate memories would recall that chairman Ray Hardman had said that was the necessary break-even figure while in the First Division, but it had taken a Premier League season to reach it.

Almost every time Swindon found a new gear to go up to, their Premier League peers also had a higher one to engage. It became apparent that the best chance that Town had of winning a match was to fight tooth and nail to keep it goalless, then strike with too little time for the opposition to respond. If you poked the bear too early and without an escape planned, it would get angry and maul you.

For some supporters the whole Premier League experience may have seemed vaguely familiar. It was like saving up for years, and looking forward to the holiday of a lifetime, then, having grown weary of watching whales or dining at the captain's table, longing for the familiarity of a mundane Marmite sandwich for tea with the rain pouring outside.

The Football League was familiar territory. Swindon Town, battered and bruised, were back where they felt at home.

6
Chapter of Legends

AS A Swindon Town supporter who lived through all the events of this book (and decades either side), the greatest privilege and pleasure of writing this story was to talk to some of those who made everything come about.

For someone who took his seat at the County Ground and watched the Robins' trials, tribulations and triumphs, who shouted, groaned, cheered and chewed his fingernails, to find the names of such heroes in his contacts list on his phone was almost surreal.

This chapter contains the thoughts and memories of some players who became heroes while plying their trade for Town. Altogether the players who have made this chapter their own made over 1,500 appearances (over 100 of them in the Premier League in 1993/94), and scored almost 300 goals between them.

To Duncan, Fraser, Paul, Shaun and Steve – thank you so much for your help, time and patience. But most of all, thank you for the most priceless gift of all: those momentous, life-punctuating memories.

Fraser Digby

Fraser first signed for Lou Macari while Swindon were still in the Fourth Division. Voted player of the year on three occasions, the England under-21 goalkeeper spent an amazing 12 seasons with the club. His 504 appearances fell four short of the previous club goalkeeping record set by Sam Burton almost 40 years previously.

DW, 'You initially signed on loan for Swindon from Manchester United in March 1986 when Town were in the Fourth Division. Did you have any first-hand knowledge of Lou Macari when you were at United?'

FD, 'No, I didn't to be fair. He was a big name at Old Trafford, but I didn't really know a lot about Lou until he later came in for me.'

DW, 'Was he influential in your decision to come to Swindon? Lou later gave the impression you were really keen.'

FD, 'Being at Manchester United for nearly four years, I'd played reserve team games, but it was always going to be difficult to get into the first team. When Lou came in for me it was an opportunity for me to play first-team football. I was keen to come on loan, and I came in for a month when Swindon were in the Fourth Division. I didn't make an appearance then and came back on loan in September. It was Lou's way of sussing me out, and it wasn't until December that I signed permanently.'

DW, 'You'd have been understudying Kenny Allen?'

FD, 'Yes, I signed on loan for the second time because Kenny was injured and I went straight into the first team. That was the only reason why Ron Atkinson would allow me to go out on loan. When Kenny got fit, I stayed in the first team and that helped me to decide to sign permanently.'

DW, 'Who was ahead of you at United?'

FD, 'Gary Bailey, Chris Turner, Jeff Wealands, Stephen Pears. Gary Walsh was a year behind me. Ron wanted a lot of money for me at the time, and it wasn't until he got the sack and Alex Ferguson came in, that things changed.'

DW, 'How much was asked?'

FD, 'It was £100,000 for someone who really hadn't done a lot. I'd played for England Schoolboys and England Youth, but only played a few reserve games at United. So, it was quite a lot of money for someone who'd not done a lot. Ron said he'd extend my loan to three months, then he got the sack. Sir Alex came in and he and Lou had a chat and did a deal.'

DW, 'It must have been a culture shock to come to Swindon.'

FD, 'Yeah, but at Manchester United I'd been a little fish in a huge pond. It was great to work with the lads, but you can't beat getting out on the pitch and playing in the first team. Swindon were getting crowds of 7,000 to 8,000 in the Third Division and it was a buzz to play in front of crowds like that.'

DW, 'Was it a shock to make the first-team shirt your own so quickly?'

FD, 'Yeah, I came in and hit the ground running and Lou was plainly pleased with it, he was happy with that. I was voted player of the year that first season. I gained England under-21 honours that year as well. It certainly was a good decision to move down.'

DW, 'Lou's fitness work must have been hard. Did you get any special dispensation for being a goalkeeper?'

FD, 'No! Not at all! We had to run the same as everybody else. Me and Nick Hammond must have been the fittest goalkeepers in the country! We didn't have a goalkeeping coach and Lou said, "You've got ability, you just need to get fit." To be fair it worked! It was amazingly successful. The players he attracted to the club is the proof of the pudding.'

DW, 'How did you get on with Nicky Hammond?'

FD, 'I spoke to Nick the other day. He's done incredibly well. He always said, "I need to do something because Fraser won't let me play!" We get on really well. We've always had a good relationship.'

DW, 'Nicky actually made more appearances than you in 1991/92.'

FD, 'I broke my thumb at Crystal Palace, and I was out for quite a while. Of course, Nick had some terrible luck with injuries, breaking a leg a couple of times.'

DW, 'Every season under Lou must have seemed to be a new challenge.'

FD, 'It was always positive. I don't think we had a negative season under Lou. We were always pushing for promotion, and it was always entertaining.'

DW, 'When Lou left and Ossie arrived, that must have been a contrast in the training routine.'

FD, 'Oh yeah! Just a little bit! The running stopped but the first time we had a goalkeeping coach was when Glenn arrived. He brought in "The Cat", Peter Bonetti, then John Gorman brought in Martin Thomas. But the training under Ossie was always enjoyable, small-sided games and "play, play, play". It was certainly more enjoyable than running round the streets of Swindon.'

DW, 'Moving on, the demotion of 1990 must have been devastating.'

FD, 'I remember where I was when I heard we'd been demoted. I was with my wife and family in a well-known Swindon Indian restaurant. We found out initially that we were getting relegated two divisions. When we got put back into the Second Division it was a slight relief. The one thing I felt was that I wished I'd had the chance to play with that squad in the top flight. The squad we had under Ossie was fantastic and I wonder just where we could have gone. The Premiership then kicked in, but the gap between divisions one and two wasn't as big then. I think we'd have had a good chance of staying at the top in 1990.'

DW, 'So, you think we'd have had a better chance staying in the First Division in 1990 than we did staying in the Premier League in 1993?'

FD, 'Yes! If Glenn and Colin Calderwood had still been playing in 1993, we might have had a better chance. John Gorman is a lovely fella but he was too nice to be a manager.

We were a bit naive. We had some fantastic performances but every mistake that was made was punished. Ultimately that cost Swindon their place in the top flight.'

DW, 'It was the biggest challenge that Swindon Town and John Gorman were ever to face.'

FD, 'That was it. Probably hearts ruled heads in the situation we were in. You couldn't wish for a better person than John to be there. Everyone was in the trenches with John, we did the best we could, but unfortunately it wasn't enough.'

DW, 'Going back to Ossie, did you detect any change in his attitude after demotion? It knocked the stuffing out of everybody, and I wonder if he felt like he was beating his head against a brick wall.'

FD, 'I think so a little bit. Sadly, he let certain people get away with things that weren't conducive to a good team spirit, and it all went away from him in the end. He gave the team so much confidence. Jon Gittens in particular never had so much confidence in his own abilities. The change in Swindon's style when Ossie arrived after Lou was like chalk and cheese. Ossie brought out everyone's ability.'

DW, 'How did it come about that you ended up understudying Peter Schmeichel at Manchester United?'

FD, 'The second full season under Glenn we played Oxford away and I didn't have the best of games. And Glenn decided to change things about. It was the first time I'd been dropped in my career. Within a week, John called me out the changing room and said he had Alex Ferguson on the phone. I said, "You're having a laugh!" But Alex was on the phone and said, "I've only got Peter Schmeichel fit. Would you come on loan?" I said, "I'll start walking now!"

'It was the best thing I could have done. I had the best two months at Old Trafford I had [in] my whole career. It gave me such a boost. When I was called back to Swindon I was recalled to the first team, again against Oxford. I had a really good game and I played all the rest of the season, all the way to beating Leicester City at Wembley. It was a turning point for me.'

DW, 'You had a consistent defence in front of you just about throughout your time at Swindon.'

FD, 'Out of all my team-mates, Colin Calderwood was the epitome of professionalism. A great lad and a great player and captain. He led by example. He was the rock in the team.'

DW, 'And complemented by Shaun Taylor.'

FD, 'Shaun was a great lad as well. He was 100 per cent committed. He'd run through a brick wall for you. They both worked so well with each other. A great combination. They were huge losses when Colin and Glenn left ahead of the Premier League season. That was a massive loss to the defence and the team as a whole. Glenn was an incredible talent even toward the end of his career. He could ping the ball 60 yards and find his man every time. He could change things and pull a team apart.'

DW, 'Wembley, 1993 – how was it for you?'

FD, 'A fantastic day. But in the end, it was one of relief rather than jubilation. We should have gone up three years prior and it was only what we deserved. We righted a wrong and it was tainted by the fact we knew Glenn was going.'

DW, 'Then reality hit in the Premier League. One hundred goals against!'

FD, 'My defence is that I was injured for quite a few months when I dislocated my shoulder at Sheffield Wednesday in December.'

DW, 'The Premier League was a crash course in reality.'

FD, 'It was. It was a steep learning curve. We went on a rollercoaster ride from the Fourth Division to the Premier League. I was at Swindon for 12 years and it was a great time to be involved. Now it's the same old names coming in and going out of the Premiership every season. It's not how it used to be.'

DW, 'Were you aware of many clubs coming in for you while you were at Swindon?'

FD, 'Not really. It was mostly paper talk. Aberdeen and QPR were mentioned at one point when David Seaman left to go to Arsenal. There was Real Madrid; I've still got the newspaper cuttings! I got up one morning and the phone was ringing and someone said, "Do you want to sit down? I understand that Real Madrid are interested in you." It was on all the back pages.'

DW, 'Was that legitimate?'

FD, 'I don't know. I never got to the bottom of it. I think Lou was under pressure at the time and he decided to deflect that. I think he said he'd spotted someone in the stand wearing a sombrero! Then Lou tried to take me to West Ham. I only found out after I'd retired that he'd offered £1m for me at the time. But the deal fell through because of Alex Ferguson. When I'd joined Swindon there had been a 50 per cent sell-on clause inserted, so Swindon would only have received 50 per cent of the fee. Brian Hiller rejected it.'

DW, 'After you'd retired you returned to Swindon as goalkeeping coach.'

FD, 'I took a call after Paolo Di Canio left [as manager in 2013] and I accepted the role of goalkeeping coach to the end of the season. At the end they said, "See you pre-season," so I stayed on without ever having any conversation about it. I had another season with Mark Cooper and then I had other options which took my time, and I decided to get out of football altogether.'

Duncan Shearer

Scottish striker Duncan was a £250,000 club record signing when he joined Swindon from Huddersfield Town in March 1986. Voted player of the year in 1990/91, he claimed an incredible average of a goal every other game over four seasons, scoring 20 league goals or more in three consecutive campaigns. Duncan went on to gain seven Scotland caps.

DW, 'You were signed by Lou Macari in 1988. What did you know about Swindon?'

DS, 'I was offered the opportunity to speak to Lou at a time when a move to West Bromwich Albion was possible. I heard from Lou a couple of days later and I believed a move to Swindon was a better move for me than one to West Brom. At the time a lot of people may have questioned my choice, but you just get a feeling sometimes and that was what I wanted to do. I must admit there were times when I wondered whether I had made the right choice, and I didn't immediately start scoring.'

DW, 'As Swindon's record signing, did that bring additional pressure?'

DS, 'It's always good as a striker to get on the scoresheet earlier to convince the fans you can score goals, because they won't take for granted that just because you have scored goals elsewhere that you are automatically going to score goals. And I didn't.

'I was disappointed in myself, and I was also disappointed in the style of play that Swindon played, which was from back to front pretty quickly, even though at the end of the season we made the play-offs. So, while on holiday I spoke to my wife and told her that the style of play didn't really suit me.

'I was going to have to ask to move on, purely because of that. Not because of the area or because of the people, but that I couldn't find a way to score goals in the style we were playing in.

'As it was, I got a tap on the shoulder on the way home from America and someone said to me, "You've lost your manager then," and Lou Macari had gone to West Ham

United. So, I decided to hang fire on the transfer request and see who came in.'

DW, 'So, if Lou hadn't left, you'd have put in a transfer request?'

DS, 'Yeah, I'd have gone in to see him and asked to move on. Nothing to do with Lou himself, it was just the style of play didn't suit me. Training was tough with all the street running. But when Ossie arrived a lot of ball players came in and the coaching became all about keeping the ball on the deck and wanting to play football.

'The thing that convinced me the most when Ossie took over was when I remember chasing the full-back down the line, and at half-time Ossie sat beside me and asked, "What are you doing? Why are you chasing the right-back everywhere? You stay up front in the box and we'll get the ball to you. That's your job. I've got other players to chase the full-back."

'I said this was news to me, and that was exactly what I'd do. You can get a reputation as a lazy player, but I was doing what I'd been told to do.

'Ossie could see what I was good at, and if I got the ball in or around the box, that I was alive to things. And when you are in a team with right- and left-backs like David Kerslake, Paul Bodin, Phil King – good things were going to happen. There wasn't a player at the club who would have said a bad thing about Ossie, that's for sure.'

DW, 'It must have been heaven-sent for you to hear your manager saying that to you, that you shouldn't waste your energy chasing and tracking back?'

DS, 'Yeah, it was good. Steve White and I were often the front partnership. I wouldn't say we linked well together and we were split up from time to time to try different things, but we always ended up together up front. We were told to play quite far apart, which allowed Alan McLoughlin to be the point of the diamond.

'With Steve and I playing towards each full-back, the centre-halves didn't know whether to follow one of us or stay in the middle, which left a lot of space for Alan. He scored a lot of goals and assisted a lot too. He'd been played out of position a lot in the past, often wide left. I remember speaking to him about it and he said he hated playing wide left. Ossie brought out the best in Alan McLoughlin.

'Credit to the board for picking the managers they did. To replace Lou with Ossie, then Ossie with Glenn. When Glenn came in, he took us a step further, and it's not easy picking a manager.'

DW, 'How do you view your partnership with Steve White?

DS, 'When we went to Wembley for the play-off final in 1990, we were sitting on 27 goals each. I told him the story that when he clipped the post in that match against Sunderland, I remember chasing the ball hoping it would come off the post so I could pop it in! I was thinking, "Hit the post, please. Don't go in!" But it rebounded the wrong way and I went arse over tit trying to knock it in!

'Chalkie was very fit, and it was nice that we both ended up on 27 goals each. We had a really good season, the two of us together.'

DW, 'The play-off defeat against Crystal Palace in 1989 must have been a low point.'

DS, 'The two strikers they had! When you are against two strikers like Mark Bright and Ian Wright, they were always going to cause all sorts of problems at the back. Palace were a really good team, but, you know, we pushed them as hard as we could.'

DW, 'The following year there was further disappointment with victory at Wembley, but then the reward of promotion to the top flight was taken away.'

DS, 'Aye. There were no medals for us either. Play-off finalists all get medals now, but we never got a thing. But some days later I came across the news of what was going to happen to us, and I thought, you are joking!

'Not only had they dropped us down from the First Division, but they also dropped us down another division too. You look back now, and you see other clubs not suffering anything like we got. But we were the little club, and we got the wrath of it. We got put back where we came from after an appeal, but it makes you wonder who makes these decisions.'

DW, 'So, on to 1990/91 and the player of the year award.'

DS, 'I remember in my first year there was some booing from a section of the fans … that's football … but I found it hard to accept. I always say that the hardest minds to change are those of the supporters, because they are stubborn in their ways. Often, they keep their assessments, regardless of what the striker does afterwards. I found it a real honour that I got the supporters' player of the year award. That I'd managed to turn them around meant more to me than winning the award itself.'

DW, 'Then in March Ossie left. More turmoil.'

DS, 'Yeah. Ossie had to cope with a lot of stuff left behind after Lou went, and for him to get hold of team spirit and sign the players he did, players who he knew would fit into the team, you couldn't begrudge him the move he got to Newcastle United.

'And then he was replaced by Glenn Hoddle, one of the best players England had ever had. When you were in training you were frightened to challenge him. He'd just drop his shoulder and he wasn't there.

'I think he found it hard though. I spoke to John Gorman about this, and he said that when Glenn was playing with Swindon, he couldn't understand why a lot of the time we weren't controlling the ball properly. He used to be quite hard on us, and he used the word "sloppy" a lot.

'John said he had a word with him and said, "Glenn. When a ball comes at you at 60 miles an hour you can kill it dead. These boys are not at the level of play that you are. You need to tone it down a bit. These boys are in this division for a reason. They are not perfect, but they are trying to be perfect. You have to help them."

'He eased off on us after that. I loved playing with Glenn.'

DW, 'Changes between Swindon under Ossie and Glenn?'

DS, 'Yeah. Glenn played himself between the centre-halves and kept slipping into the midfield, switching the ball around. His passing was fantastic. There were some though who thought, hang on, you're getting a bit old now, but he was in the team because he was our best player. Not only did we get a good manager, we got a very good player too. There has to be a lot of credit to John Gorman as well. He was a fantastic coach.'

DW, So, football today. Has it changed for the better?'

DS, 'For the players it has, yes. I'm not sure about for the fans.'

DW, 'Do you suffer VAR in Scotland?'

DS, 'Yeah. I was a big advocate when it came in. Now I'm not so sure. Officials will always make honest mistakes. We're all human beings. But we still seem to be arguing even with VAR. Why don't we just scrap it and go back to the way we were?'

DW, 'In March 1992 you moved on to Blackburn Rovers. Did this take you by surprise?'

DS, 'I think it did. It wasn't expected that Swindon wanted to sell anyone, but it seemed that the club needed some money quickly. Glenn told me there had been a few offers for other players, but the thing about the one for me was that it was straight cash. Normally transfers are paid in stages, so the offer of all the money up front was attractive to Swindon.

'I was actually going to sign for Notts County. I'd spoken to their manager Neil Warnock at their chairman's house, they'd made me an offer and I said, "Let me go back and speak to my wife. I'm very keen to come."

'The next day I spoke to Glenn to say I was going to Notts County, and he told me there had been a development from Blackburn Rovers and that Kenny Dalglish wanted me. Kenny was my boyhood hero.

'So, I spoke to Neil Warnock and said I was on my way to speak to Kenny Dalglish, and he said, "Well that's the end of that then."

'Soon after I joined Blackburn, we all went to Balmoral, and Gordon Cowans said to me, "We're in the play-off positions now and we're just grateful you came away from Swindon." Swindon had already beaten Blackburn easily that season, but now both teams were in the play-off positions, and he said, "We wanted you out of their team."'

DW, 'It's always been believed in Swindon that Blackburn owner Jack Walker's money was used tactically to deny Swindon your goalscoring abilities, with both teams challenging for a play-off place.'

DS, 'I was told that. Soon after Blackburn won the play-offs and promotion, I was told there were a couple of teams who were interested in me and if I wanted to go, I was more than welcome to walk away.'

DW, 'You must have felt used.'

DS, 'I did, yes. But I was at the stage in my career when I needed to plan my future and certainly the move to Blackburn was financially good for me to add to my pension. When you get to an age when you haven't made a fortune out of football and you have the chance to treble your wages, it's difficult to turn it down. I get where today's players are coming from, when they go to Saudi Arabia or somewhere lucrative.

'But I've got a lot of good memories from my time with Swindon.'

Steve White

Once a record signing for Luton Town, Chipping Sodbury-born Steve was signed from Bristol Rovers by Lou Macari on a free transfer in 1986 and went on to score the brace of goals which brought the Third Division play-off final victory over Gillingham in 1987. Six seasons later it was the challenge on him at Wembley that brought the penalty despatched by Paul Bodin to claim Premier League promotion. In total White played well over 300 times for Town and is a member of the prestigious and exclusive band of players who scored more than 200 league goals over his career.

DW, 'Thanks for talking. I've already spoken to Shaun Taylor, Duncan Shearer and Paul Bodin and I've enjoyed our chats.'

SW, 'Old footballers love talking about football because they have never done anything better in their lives. I signed for Lou Macari to join Swindon, and he was fantastic for my career. I loved him.'

DW, 'Didn't everybody?'

SW, 'Those who couldn't run didn't! My room-mate Zippy never enjoyed the running but technically he was outstanding, and a superb player. That he went on to gain 23 Welsh caps shows just how good he was.'

DW, 'Just how did Paul Bodin acquire the nickname Zippy? Was it anything to do with his speed on the wing? Or perhaps a perverse reference to the character on children's TV programme *Rainbow* alongside Bungle?'

SW, 'Neither! One Sunday morning, Lou Macari unexpectedly called us all in for extra training. Paul seemed to have had an enjoyable evening the night before and appeared to be suffering from the consequences. Lou, perhaps suspicious of Paul's previous indulgences, was unimpressed with his enthusiasm and questioned, "Come on Paul! Where's your zip?" From then on, every time a ball was played to Paul the shout of "Zippy!" went up.'

DW, 'And the nickname Baldrick you used post-match at Wembley 1993?'

SW, 'Well, that was banter to the fact that Zippy's hairline was already creeping higher.'

DW, 'I tried to contact Jan-Åge Fjørtoft.'

SW, 'He can chat for England! Highly intelligent. Micky Hazard was also a fantastic player technically. A superb player.'

DW, 'I will be referencing Shaun Close in the book.'

SW, 'A nice lad. Always respectful. Polite. I had the impression he really didn't want to be at Swindon. Perhaps as a Londoner he was homesick. He was there to further his footballing career. He had a great touch, good with his back to goal, but of course as a forward if you don't score goals, you are under pressure.'

DW, 'Among Glenn's first signings was striker Dave Mitchell. He played the first couple of games of 1991/92 and then got injured. You took his place and scored 15 times. When Mitchell was fit again, he regained his place. Did you feel you'd become the third-choice striker?'

SW, 'No. That's when I had my back injury. I remember going to Derby County and Glenn Hoddle pulling me over and asking, "When are you going to be fit, Steve, because the team is missing you badly?" It was then that he sent me to see faith healer Eileen Drewery. Glenn believed in her, but he told me it was my choice, and I thought, why not? This was before MRI scans, and I'd never had any real injuries in my career. Regular osteopaths and chiropractors hadn't worked.

'Finally, I found that two of my bottom spinal discs were poking into my spinal cord. I couldn't feel my left ankle. I was out for six to eight months, had a revolutionary injection and I've never had any trouble since.

'Dave Mitchell was a great athlete and was signed for his speed, but I never felt under pressure as such. I knew I could score goals. Then Glenn signed Craig Maskell, who was a very good signing and technically sound. Of course, he scored against Tranmere Rovers in both legs of the play-off semi-final and scored a marvellous goal against Leicester City in the final at Wembley.'

DW, 'With mention of the momentous play-off final win, I have to ask something that Shaun Taylor had asked me to bring up. With my tongue firmly in my cheek – was it a penalty?'

SW, 'I've been asked that question a thousand times! I was on the bench at Wembley because I'd been sent off at Brentford for the only time in my career. Once in 750 games! I went up for a ball against Keith Millen and accidentally struck him with my elbow. I never intentionally did such a thing in my career.

'Keith wrote to the FA saying it was a complete accident, but they still wouldn't rescind it. Keith was a lovely lad, and it was a complete accident. So, I lost my place at Wembley and Craig Maskell took my place.'

DW, 'You and Duncan Shearer had a great partnership.'

SW, 'I do reunions with Luton every six months. When I was there, there was me, Brian Stein and David Moss; 57 goals in one season! That was a brilliant team. Ricky Hill was the best player I ever played with after Glenn Hoddle.

'But going on to the Swindon team [in 1989/90] of Shearer and myself, there was Alan McLoughlin playing in the front of the diamond. Alan had 16 goals and Duncan and myself had 53 between us. That doesn't happen these days, maybe because so many teams play with just one centre-forward and two wide players.'

DW, 'Alan McLoughlin became a revelation. He seemed destined to be a defender.'

SW, 'He was signed by Lou Macari at 19 and he was so nervous. It was Ossie who made him into a front-of-diamond midfielder.'

DW, 'Just how did he spot that potential?'

SW, 'A masterstroke! A very clever man, Ossie Ardiles. How did he suss that one out? He also sussed out that Ross MacLaren couldn't play anywhere else but sitting holding the diamond because, while technically his range of passing was outstanding, he couldn't get around the pitch. But his passing range was fantastic.

'Also, Jon Gittens wasn't technically as good as Colin Calderwood, but he could catch pigeons! Nobody could outrun him. Ossie knew that if Colin got caught in possession, Gittens would get back. So, with MacLaren sitting deep, Kerslake and Bodin as wing-backs being encouraged to push on all the time, and with Tom Jones and Steve Foley, both excellent players in midfield and McLoughlin behind the front two … it was a great team! They always say that that team would have survived in the top flight.'

DW, 'You plainly stayed connected with the locality in which you had grown up. Did you feel comfortable when your career took you to the metropolis with Luton and Charlton? Had you felt like a fish out of water?'

SW, 'No! I would have gone anywhere in the country to play football. I am an A licence coach, managed Chippenham Town for five years and once applied for the Swindon Town manager's job, but coaching never gave me that absolute satisfaction that I found in playing, competing and scoring goals. That was my real passion.

'I was four years in London. Luton signed me for £200,000, a club record fee at the time. I was on a five-year contract, and when I was just two and a half years in and I'd just scored 20 goals and we'd won promotion to the First Division, manager David Pleat called me into the office to say that Charlton Athletic wanted to sign me.

'The plan was for Paul Walsh to travel in the opposite direction as part of the deal. Luton were about to go into the First Division, and I said, "I'm not going anywhere!" Then Liverpool came in for Walsh which apparently scuppered the whole deal. Pleat told me I could stay … but that I wasn't going to play!

'What happened in the end was that Pleat arranged for me to meet Charlton manager Ken Craggs at the Ritz Hotel; he persuaded me to sign a contract there and then. What I didn't know was that Walsh, who hadn't gone to Liverpool, had been contacted again by Pleat. It was a part-exchange deal, and had I known, Pleat knew I wouldn't have signed.

'So, I'm going up in the lift, and I meet Walsh coming down. We exchanged pleasantries and it was obvious what was going on. We both just laugh about it now, but it wasn't funny at the time.'

DW, 'It always surprised me that despite scoring so freely at Luton and Charlton, they both sold you. And that Bristol Rovers gave you a free!'

SW, 'When I went back to Rovers the supporters didn't accept me like they did the first time. [Prolific forward] Paul Randall was loved by them and when the finances got tight, anyone on decent money had to go. I was just fortunate to talk to Lou Macari, and John Trollope played a massive part in me joining Swindon Town. The free transfer did me a massive favour. I had eight fantastic years at Swindon, five of which brought play-off participation.

'In 1987 we beat Gillingham at Crystal Palace to gain promotion to the Second Division, and in 1989 we lost in the semi-final against Crystal Palace. We beat then 1-0 at home. I had a goal disallowed off the crossbar which bounced over the line, and the ref didn't give it. And the rows I was having with Ian Wright! He was nasty at the time. That would have made it 2-0. Then they beat us 2-0 at Selhurst Park and went to Wembley 2-1 on aggregate.'

DW, 'And continuing on the play-off theme, what of that 4-3 Wembley victory that took Swindon to the Premier League in 1993?'

SW, 'I didn't answer that question you asked about the penalty. That's the first question every Swindon supporter asks. I came on as a sub … I didn't take penalties … if I could have gone round the goalkeeper and taken the glory myself, do you really think I wouldn't have done it? Kevin Poole spun me around, just as I'd seen him do to Shaun Taylor earlier, and it was definitely a penalty. But if it had gone to extra time, I think we may have lost, because we were spent.'

DW, 'But after Leicester came back from 3-0 down, we had a resurgence!'

SW, 'After I came back from suspension at Brentford, I turned an ankle in training. Physio Kevin Morris had ten days to get me fit and I had an ice boot on three times a day. No running. And on my third run at Wembley my hamstring went. How I got through the day I don't know. But what a fantastic day!'

Paul Bodin

Welsh international left-back Paul Bodin first signed for Swindon in March 1988 and played nine seasons across two spells at the County Ground. Appearing almost 300 times in total for the Robins, his penalty at Wembley clinched Town's promotion to the Premier League in 1993. Unsurprisingly, Paul was recognised as Swindon's player of the year at the end of that season.

DW, 'I know you are still regularly seen around the County Ground.'

PB, 'I still enjoy watching Swindon Town although a lot of the old faces have moved on. Relegation looks to have been avoided now. Ian Holloway took his time to get to know his players and things are looking a lot better.'

DW, 'Holloway is so old-school and a breath of fresh air.'

PB, 'He tells it as it is. He's got old-school values which are still important. He's not caught up with all the thinking that it's more important to have more passes than to score more goals.'

DW, 'Surely you have to have the players who are capable of playing in the style that you are coaching them?'

PB, 'Absolutely. When Ossie Ardiles took over from Lou Macari we went from a direct, power-driven style to a South American-influenced diamond formation.

'You can be lucky when you sign for a new club. You're never too sure how it will turn out. I was at Newport County at the time, who were in financial trouble. I was only there six weeks and Swindon had almost signed me before I went there from Bath City.

'I did some homework on Swindon Town when Lou Macari rang, and I was up the motorway the next day, signing straight away. Not much negotiation was necessary, and I'm absolutely delighted that I've stayed in the area ever since.

'It was a fantastic move. I spent eight years as a player then went into the coaching side. To achieve the success, reach the Premiership and to play at Wembley twice was incredible for me and all my team-mates. There were no bad apples in the group. Lou did all the recruitment, and he was brilliant at that, then Ossie took the footballing side to the next level, signing David Kerslake and Micky Hazard. Then Glenn took us to the level above that with his own style and with very few new players. All three need to take huge credit for continuing to build upon the success.'

DW, 'The changes in training regimes between all three of them must have been a big culture shock?'

PB, 'It was incredible. Lou's style was direct, wearing the opposition out. We were famous for our long training runs up Marlborough Downs … Barbury Castle … some players really enjoyed it, but I didn't particularly enjoy the six-mile runs.'

DW, 'Did Fraser Digby do the long runs too?'

PB, 'Absolutely. He was as fit as a fiddle as well. On two or three Thursdays a month we did a 5.7-mile run with everyone trying to beat each other and their own personal best. Ross MacLaren was one of those who didn't like them and perhaps his role didn't need him to have that level of fitness. Ross was a fantastic passer of the ball and his role relative to Glenn's meant that they could interchange on the pitch.'

DW, 'So, when Lou left and Ossie came in, those 5.7-mile runs finished?'

PB, 'Oh yes! Lou was offered the chance to go to Chelsea but went to West Ham United, and I must give him credit for all the fantastic work he's subsequently doing for homeless people with the Macari Foundation in Stoke.

'Ossie's appointment as Lou's replacement came out of the blue. To change to his style of play was incredible. It built so much confidence in us, it was a pleasure. The long runs stopped immediately. We did shorter, sharper work … five-a-sides … a huge transformation. We started playing in a diamond shape and Alan McLoughlin, God rest his soul, excelled in the number ten role. His goals, added to Duncan Shearer's and Steve White's, produced an incredible total. Ossie's guidance allowed his ability to come to fruition, and the same could be said with Ross MacLaren.

'With two narrow midfielders in Steve Foley and Tom Jones in front of me, I had to learn to cope facing two-on-ones. I would track the runner and force him to cross 10 or 15 yards from the penalty box. If that meant we forfeited some defensive exposure, we gained on our quality of forward play, and under Ossie we always thought we would outscore the opposition anyway.

'Lou held a tight rein. He would check up on us in the evening and at the team hotel at away games. In contrast Ossie trusted everyone implicitly. Then, on a Saturday after a game, as husbands and wives we would go out in Old Town. Shaun [Taylor], [Martin] Lingy, Moncs [John Moncur], Tom Jones ... we enjoyed it and the interaction with locals was good. Only recently, somebody asked to shake my hand and thanked me for scoring *that* penalty.

'Under Ossie I signed three contracts. Phil King always tells me that it was down to him that I got into the team as left-back when he left for Sheffield Wednesday. Until then I played mainly in midfield but when he left, I established myself at left-back. When we're together now at events and we're asked who was Swindon Town's best left-back, we always say John Trollope!'

DW, 'I've discovered that you were on the schoolboy books of Chelsea.'

PB, 'Yes. I was playing for my local youth club in Wales when two gentlemen introduced themselves as Chelsea scouts and said, "We'd like you to go to Chelsea on trial." They met my mum and asked my school's permission to travel on Fridays. As a 14-year-old, I'd catch a bus to Cardiff, take a train to Paddington, the tube and a taxi to a hotel owned by Ray Wilkins' mum and dad. I first met Tom Jones there. I did the trip every weekend and stayed there every holiday for two years.

'I'd train, watch Chelsea's first team play and then travel back. It was amazing. The world was very different then regarding the risks kids would take. But I didn't get taken on as an apprentice, although Tom did.

'I went non-league initially, then chose Newport County in favour of Cardiff City when the opportunity came along. Newport were playing in the European Cup Winners' Cup quarter-finals against Carl Zeiss Jena at the time, which they qualified for by winning the Welsh Cup. County manager Len Ashurst believed in me, and when he left for Cardiff, he took me with him.'

DW, 'In March 1991 you left Swindon for Crystal Palace. How did that come about?'

PB, 'We'd been demoted after winning at Wembley and we'd had the stuffing knocked out of us. Swindon were always a selling club if the price was right. Palace were doing really well under Steve Coppell at the time, and it was a good choice. Training was about power running and 30-minute, 11-a-side matches. It was a wonderful opportunity.

'The transfer was structured so that once I'd played 15 games, Palace had to pay Swindon an extra sum … £250,000 I think, and I didn't know that at the time. I got to 14 appearances and got stuck. By the time the next season started, Palace had signed Chris Coleman and my chance had gone. I spoke to the manager and chairman Ron Noades, who explained they didn't want to pay the extra fee and I could go out on loan.'

DW, 'Did you feel let down?'

PB, 'Yeah, Steve Coppell was a very quiet man and it was Alan Smith who told me, then Ron Noades confirmed it.

Palace had paid a fee for Coleman, similar to the extra that was due for me.

'I joined Newcastle United in December to rejoin Ossie Ardiles, as part of a swap deal that was to take Franz Carr to Selhurst. The intention was that we'd both sign permanent deals after the loan deals had run their course. But Carr fractured his kneecap and the permanent deals fell apart. I really enjoyed my spell at Newcastle, a fantastic club which had financial trouble at the time, then Glenn came in to take me back to Swindon. We still had our house in Swindon, so I thought, yeah, let's go home.'

DW, 'It must have felt great for your confidence that someone the calibre of Glenn Hoddle wanted you, and that you'd also be able to return to somewhere you by now counted as home.'

PB, 'Yes. And it was the manager who did most things then, rather than today when it would be handled by a director or the head of recruitment, etc. They were great days at Swindon. Lou was a footballing legend, Ossie was a World Cup winner and Glenn was one of England's greatest ever midfielders, so to have those three players coaching you was crazy, and it was all happening at Swindon Town.'

DW, 'When you left Swindon again in 1996, Steve McMahon was the manager.'

PB, 'We had just won the Second Division title and at Christmas I'd been told to expect a new contract offer. By then we'd signed another left-back in Jason Drysdale, but he suffered a series of injuries and I continued to play over 30 matches that season. The season was finished, and I was on my way to play golf with Mark Seagraves, when I got a call that Steve wanted to talk to me. When I reached the office at the County Ground, I found the expected contract offer wasn't to be tabled. It was the same for Shaun Taylor and Lingy. We all loved being at Swindon Town.'

DW, 'You'll always be remembered for your penalties.'

PB, 'Early on I'd always been a midfielder or striker, and I was playing for Cardiff schoolboys one night, ironically at Swindon, when our left-back was injured. I was asked to play left-back for the first time, and I scored two goals. Chelsea were watching because I was on their books, and they then switched me to left-back as well, so that was where I stayed. I always enjoyed getting forward and scoring, and I was quite a good passer of the ball, and I found I enjoyed taking penalties. I was confident and more than happy taking them.'

DW, 'Well thanks for scoring the most important spot kick in Swindon Town's history! But soon afterwards, there was a different outcome from 12 yards for Wales.'

PB, 'Yeah. That's the one that gets talked about in Wales! At the time I'd taken three for Wales and scored them all. We needed to win against Romania and they only needed to draw. At around the 60th minute I had the chance to put us in front. I struck it well, it hit the crossbar and came back out. But I played for my country having been brought up on a council estate and having been released twice as a youngster. I'm proud of what I achieved. I was disappointed to miss that one, but I'm more than proud to say I scored the one at Wembley to take Swindon to the Premiership.'

DW, 'Was that the pinnacle, to score at Wembley and go on to play in the Premier League?'

PB, 'Yes. Kicking a ball around as a kid, I always dreamed that every goal was at Wembley, so to actually go through it for real, fulfilled all those dreams.'

Shaun Taylor

Another man to have been voted Swindon's player of the year three times, central defender Shaun was a colossus at the back across 260 league outings. Always ready to give his all for his club, often while bandaged or stitched, Shaun was on the scoresheet in the play-off final of 1993, being ever-present in the Premier League season.

DW, 'You must have been considered a hero by the supporters of all the clubs you played for. They would have seen something of themselves in you.'

ST, 'I played thinking people had paid to watch all 22 players, and I always thought I was working. I didn't have an apprenticeship because I came up the non-league way and to me that was the better way, to go through the leagues. I'd grown up seeing all the aspects of football to get to the top, and in a way I'm quite proud of that. I thought that perhaps I had missed my opportunity, and I felt that if I was to get a second chance, I knew I had to put the effort in.'

DW, 'Did that make it all the sweeter when Swindon made the Premier League?'

ST, 'Yes, and in one game I managed to do all the things I wanted to do as a professional footballer. Play at Wembley, score at Wembley and go on to play in the Premiership. I'd done all of them. Obviously, I'd always wanted to play professionally and obviously I'd have liked to have played longer in the top league. I know Swindon supporters still talk about that season and even though we lost a lot of games it was a fantastic time.'

DW, 'I've read that before you signed for Swindon in 1991 you had impressed in a trial against Spurs with the club in 1985. What do you remember about that?'

ST, 'No, I don't remember that at all. Terry Cooper was my manager at Exeter City and while I was there, I went to Norwich City and Hibernian for trials, and I also went to Ipswich, but I'm pretty sure I would have remembered going to Swindon. I've never heard that mentioned before.'

DW, 'I thought that was strange. In May 1985 you'd have been at Bideford Town, and attracting interest from professional clubs, but you didn't sign for Exeter for a further 18 months.'

ST, 'Yes. The reason I signed for Exeter was that for financial reasons all the Bideford players' contracts were cancelled. Exeter rang to offer me a month's trial as a free agent. Two weeks in they gave me a contract. I can't ever remember going to Swindon until I signed six years later.'

DW, 'What was training under Glenn Hoddle like?'

ST, 'Obviously Glenn was player as well as manager, with John Gorman taking the weight off his shoulders, and he came to Swindon from Chelsea. I wanted to be in his team, and I saw what he could do. For me to be in his side, as a "bustling" centre-half, and not being the most skilful of players, I couldn't do the sort of things that he could do.

'We did sessions on technique and those improved me immensely, improved my ability ten-fold being on the same training pitch as Glenn and having those sessions on all things. Being cynical I thought he just wanted me to head the ball and I would have looked out of place if I couldn't do the sort of things that I eventually could. My previous training would have been tackling, aggression, trapping, passing … but all Colin Calderwood and I had to do was get the ball and give it to Glenn.'

DW, 'Did you immediately strike up a good rapport with Colin Calderwood?'

ST, 'Everyone got on really well. Our families all got on well and it was all very close-knit. There was Paul Bodin, Colin Calderwood, Martin Ling … we all socialised. Colin had been there a while when I joined, and when you go to a new club you have to earn that right to be in the team. I worked hard and it was gradual, but when you work with nice and better people you are going to get better.'

DW, 'You were incredibly consistent in your appearances throughout your time with Exeter City and Swindon.'

ST, 'I was ... until I broke my collarbone at Bristol City after I left Swindon.'

DW, 'Looking back at the final against Leicester, what do you think happened between Swindon going 3-0 up and being dragged back to 3-3?'

ST, 'On the day, when we were winning, all you could hear was Swindon fans. So, 3-0 and coasting, then as Leicester started scoring, all you could hear was Leicester fans, even though both sets of fans were cheering as loudly as ever. For them to come back to 3-3, they had put so much effort into it they were drained. With 20 minutes to go in the game we had two or three good chances, and we turned the tide again. Even then we thought it would go to extra time. Then Steve White got brought down, Paul Bodin tucked away the penalty and you couldn't put into words how we felt.

'It all summed up our season really. There was a game at Birmingham where we won 6-4. I went off injured, and in the treatment room for some stitches I was told we were 1-0 down. So, I said, "Can you hurry up?" Then we went 2-0 down, I came back on and scored to make it 2-1. Glenn gave us the spiel at half-time, and then we went 4-1 down! And we eventually won 6-4!

'That was when the manager really came into his own. He changed things around, pushed himself into midfield so we were stretched at the back. But we won 6-4. Ironically, by then Terry Cooper was manager of Birmingham City and my wife and I went out for a meal with Terry and his wife afterwards. It was a bit embarrassing!

'But going back to the Wembley game, we scored lots of goals and conceded our fair share that season, but the way we played we were always going to score more than the other team.'

DW, 'The eventual outcome of the Premier League season was a big disappointment, but was it totally unexpected?'

ST, 'We all tried our best, but it was probably proof that as a team and as individuals we were not good enough. We lost a lot of key players in the summer and for financial reasons didn't replace them with similar ones. I thoroughly enjoyed every minute. But we did it, and I probably would not have got there playing for any other team. Now the Premier League is like a revolving door with the same teams up and down all the time.'

DW, 'At the time Swindon were saddled with all sorts of Premier League records, although the Premier League was only two seasons old.'

ST, 'A lot of those records are diminishing as they get beaten. Only the 100 goals against remains … and that wasn't for the lack of trying.'

DW, 'Are there any particular opponents or specific matches that stick in your mind of the Premier League season?'

ST, 'Ian Wright, Ian Rush, Peter Beardsley, Alan Shearer … all of them! It sometimes felt strange that I was in their company, but I knew I deserved to be there. I kept copious books of my playing and coaching sessions and when I stopped coaching and moved house I must have had ten boxes of paperwork. I kept a programme for every game I played in, and I had a bonfire and burned almost everything, except those that related to that Premier League season … particularly pictures.'

DW, 'What are your memories of the period when Steve McMahon replaced John Gorman as manager?'

ST, 'It was difficult and the reason I left Swindon Town. There was an agreement in pre-season that I would be offered a new contract, but Rikki Hunt, the chairman, soon told me of interest from Bristol City. I was happy in Swindon and so were my wife and family. It was obviously important that at the age of 34 or 35 that I needed to play. I spoke to Joe Jordan, manager of Bristol City, and agreed to join them. It was September and I never had the chance to say my goodbyes. It wasn't that I wanted to go.

'When we won the Second Division in 1996 the crowd were shouting my name, and all the other players' names. Before I left Swindon, I was told that my legs had gone, but I played for another two or three years at Bristol City. Then I did my cruciate ligament, and even then I managed another 18 months or so. I thought it a bit odd to be offered a new contract pre-season at Swindon, and then to be told an approach for me from Bristol City had been accepted. I didn't want to go. I had another year on my contract.'

DW, 'The first image of you that any Swindon supporter will bring to mind is one with you wearing a bandage on your head. It has become your cult image! Were you concerned about the potential of long-term damage?'

ST, 'You wouldn't get away with that now. Training was all about heading for me. I headed more balls in training than

I ever did on matchdays. I did go to Oxford for a scan, and I have had various tests, but I feel good and, touch wood, I'm OK. I wanted to win by all fair means, and I only ever had two red cards. The first was at Bideford after a bit of pushing and shoving, and the second was at Bristol City when the ball hit my hand and prevented a goal. I was never sent off at Swindon. I don't like the grabbing that goes on at corners and free kicks these days, when players don't even look at the ball, only at their opponents.'

DW, 'So, do you think football today is worse to watch and play?'

ST, 'If they ever took heading out of the game, it wouldn't be a proper game of football any more. I was always told that if I went up for a corner or free kick I was going there to score a goal. Today the commitment to score doesn't appear to be there as much. Why go up? It's right to limit heading with kids, but professionals need to practise to get better.'

Afterword

SWINDON TOWN'S rise to the Premier League had begun with the arrival of Lou Macari as player-manager in 1984 while the club were scrapping in the basement division, and when the competition was still little more than an aspiration of the power- and cash-hungry top clubs in the country.

Under the Scot, the Robins had achieved successive promotions and established themselves as a credible force in the Second Division, failing to reach the First Division at the play-off stage in 1989.

First Ossie Ardiles and then Glenn Hoddle conspired to realise the dream of top-flight football at the County Ground in 1993, bringing with it glory, reward, disappointment and ultimately heartbreak. But huge adventure.

Over the following three decades a belief that football was invented in 1992 has developed. A belief that over a century played under the auspices of the Football League didn't count for anything, almost as if the Football League was a prototype and a poor relation for what was destined to follow.

To some that seems incredibly dismissive of more than 100 years of history and achievement. Records, such as Huddersfield Town's three consecutive title-winning years in the 1920s, seem to have been rendered irrelevant.

Discussions regarding English football's records today all seem to be qualified as 'the first time in Premier League history'. Football, or at least the media, has become disrespectful to all that happened before the Premier League was formed.

So, when Swindon joined the Premier League in 1993, one season after it had been founded, the only team who had 'ever' won the title were Manchester United. Virtually all records were there to be set, and Town supporters raised wry, weary eyebrows when they were told that no club other than theirs had been relegated from the Premier League with as few points as 30.

History had only just begun.

It was a record which lasted one season, when Ipswich Town were relegated with 27.

Swindon fans were also told that no other club had conceded 100 goals in Premier League history. That record has lasted the test of time (so far) although Southampton, relegated on 12 points in 2025, looked likely to push the goals against column into treble figures all season, finishing on 86, having played four games fewer than Swindon had in 1993/94.

Swindon's top-flight adventure came after 114 years of trying, and that the top level had recently been redefined as the Premier League was at the time in many ways incidental.

But today, because of the divide that has been driven through the ranks of football since its inception, the likelihood of a club the size and financial wherewithal of Swindon reaching the top level seems more remote than ever.

That a club like the Robins could rise through four divisions over ten years and reach the top was the very essence of the romance of football. That seems to have died, and football is all the poorer because of it.

Acknowledgements

WHAT IS essentially a chronology of the times of a football club is enhanced considerably by the input from five legendary names in the history of Swindon Town. I've spoken to authentic West Country heroes, international cap winners, record goalscorers, massive appearance makers and fabled defenders of dreams.

My thanks go to Duncan, Fraser, Paul, Shaun and Steve for their time and patience in supplying the content for 'Chapter of Legends'. Without their memories this book would not contain the personal reminiscences of people responsible for so many supporters' greatest moments.

Paul's extra contribution of a foreword to introduce the whole thing is particularly appreciated. Cheers again, Paul.

Not for the first time, fellow Swindon sufferer Phil Leslie offered much valued support, advice and professional judgement as his eagle eye spotted the silly mistakes that are inevitable from months of often feverish keyboard bashing. Thanks once more for the enthusiasm and encouragement, Phil. Any remaining mistakes are the result of my subsequent tinkering.

Big thanks are due to Joe Acklam at the *Swindon Advertiser* for his help searching the local newspaper's archives, and to the editor Daniel Chipperfield for allowing access to, and use of, pictures and references. Those images would not be available at all without the sterling work of long-term photographer Dave Evans who I thank, not for the first time, for his professional output.

Swindon Town media man Callum Knowles helpfully advised the acceptability to use some words from the club's matchday programme, for which I am very grateful.

If I have missed anyone out in my thanks for their help and contribution to this book, please accept my apologies. The passage of more than 30 years may have blurred the traceability of some sources.

As with my previous work, my acknowledgement of the effort that Richard Banyard and Paul Plowman put in to construct the excellent Swindon Town website TownEnders.com, which is an invaluable source of detail for anyone interested in our club. The availability of such information makes writing about the Robins hugely less taxing and the research vastly more entertaining.

My grateful thanks go to all the talented team at Pitch Publishing for their work in turning 66,000 words into a book. I hope the quality of the telling of the story reflects the professionalism demonstrated in their finished product.

Writing about Swindon Town has been an obsession of mine for some decades, and brings great satisfaction. But doing so is rendered relatively pointless unless someone out there shares my passion for the subject matter and can be bothered to read it. If you are one of those people, thank you.

Finally thank you to all my fellow supporters who fill the County Ground seats, travel the motorways and spend their precious time and money following our club. Without us, STFC would have no reason to exist.

Whatever the result, keep the faith.

About the Author

DAVID WALLIS had the misfortune to be born in Surrey, clearly the victim of some sort of Douglas Adams-esque cosmic joke. 'Nobody asked me!' the plainly mislocated Wiltshire Moonraker remembers protesting to his parents, as they finally relented and moved the family to Swindon – where he belonged – when he was ten.

Over 50 years later he has established himself in rural Wiltshire for over half his life, but in between came something that was far more significant than mere geography.

A first trip to the County Ground to watch Swindon Town before the 1960s expired brought about a love affair that has now almost surpassed 60 years.

After 50 years as a Town season ticket holder, far too much time, money, emotion and, well everything really, has been invested in all things Robins. Holidays, parties, family events, even his wedding have all been arranged around the fixture list.

Career potentials have been restricted by their vicinity to the County Ground. House moves have been dictated by the distance to travel on a matchday.

Early midweek college courses were chosen, only after careful cross-referencing to regular home midweek fixtures. One evening exam was cut short to enable a pre-kick-off arrival at the County Ground for an unexpected League

Cup replay (Swindon beat Stoke City 2-1, Ray McHale and Alan Mayes scored the goals, David can only guess that he must have passed the exam).

Most people will be bewildered how anyone can allow a football club to dictate so much about their lives. But those are the people who are less likely to be reading a book like this. Those who are reading just might understand better.

Can you identify with a Swindon Town obsessive?

This is David's third book on his club. He thinks he really must get out more.

Burma
Burmah